'To unlock the power of your relationship with your child for all th

– Professor Tanya Byron, consultant clinical psychologist, author, journalist and broadcaster

'When can I do [the conversations] again?'

– Imogen, age 5

'This book made me remember all the happy things and think about things differently. It was really fun.'

– Elliot, age 10

'This book provides a wonderful way for me and my son to connect, remember and celebrate our special times and work through the tough ones. A beautiful and playful tool for unlocking feelings without drama.'

– Peter Drake, Elliot's dad

'What a wonderful book, suitable for any (and all!) parents and carers, to help you build a closer relationship with your child through conversations. The authors draw upon years of clinical psychology practice of supporting young people and families, to identify creative, fun conversation starters and concepts, which can help all parents and carers to develop more meaningful connections with their child, and better understand their child's inner world. This book is compassionate and compelling and acknowledges how tricky it can be sometimes be for all parents and carers to "find a way in" with their child. It gives copious, helpful, wide-ranging advice. I will certainly be buying a copy, and highly recommending the book to parents, carers, families, professionals and everyone!'

– Dr Sue Knowles, consultant clinical psychologist, lead for child and family services at Changing Minds UK, researcher and author

'While the art of conversation is not easy for autistic children, the incredible conversation activities in this excellent book, will facilitate mutual understanding, self-reflection and emotion regulation. Although this book was primarily written for parents, I strongly recommend that psychologists, therapists and teachers incorporate the activities in their work with children who have communication difficulties.'

– Tony Attwood, professor of clinical psychology, Griffith University, and author

'Perhaps the most valuable lessons we can give our children are how to develop and maintain good relationships, as the correlation between healthy and good relationships, and success and happiness is indisputable. This book takes that rather daunting responsibility and breaks it down into clear, fun and eminently doable practices that can be weaved into everyday life...considerably reducing the number of "How was your day?" – "Fine" conversations! Moreover, whilst this book will certainly help the child–parent communication experience, its learnings can be applied to all relationships, which is why I have copies on my coffee, kitchen and bedside tables!'

— Beth Kerr, Group Director of Wellbeing for global schools group Cognita

'Following up on their incredibly successful book about the teenage brain, these authors have now turned their attention to slightly younger children and the critical issue of social communication in the family. Their aim is to lay down a road map, showing parents how to talk to their children, without either patronising them or scolding them. Do we really need to be told how to converse with pre-adolescent boys and girls? From the scientific evidence these experienced clinicians have gathered, the answer is a resounding "yes". Social communication skills are the bedrock of social and emotional development. If we don't learn to listen to others, and respond appropriately, mutually satisfying social relationships will forever elude us. Those skills should have their foundations laid down in early childhood. All parents and children would benefit from reading this "how to" guide together.'

— David Skuse, Professor of Developmental Neuropsychiatry, University College London

'I thought it was going to be a bit like homework...but it was much fun-er...the conversations make me feel good about myself...and anyone can do them!'

– Alfie, age 11

'His answers made me smile.'

— Sam Sanson (Alfie's Mum)

'Have you ever wondered how you could improve the conversations you have with your child? If so, this is the resource for you (and your child!). Firmly based in sound scientific evidence, and informed by years of clinical psychology practice, but not coming across as such, this is an extremely readable guide, full of valuable tips for having successful conversations. These in turn will build better relationships. We are advised to grasp those moments when you least expect your child to express an idea or worry and "If you can, stop what you are doing, switch off your phone, sit down and listen", I would strongly recommend (if you can) stopping what you are doing, switching off your phone and making time to read this absorbing book.'

— Helen Bedford, Professor of Children's Health, Co-Director of Education,
UCL Great Ormond Street Institute of Child Health

'This is a truly practical book full of imaginative ideas for intriguing conversations specifically designed to build parent–child relationships and foster good communication. The conversation topics have been carefully chosen to help children learn to talk about emotions safely and express opinions thoughtfully, and to help parents learn to listen and connect. It is full of useful prompts to guide parents away from monosyllabic cul-de-sacs so we can co-create authentic conversations jointly with our children. After just one of these conversations, you will understand your child a little better and build a relationship in which they feel more confident to open up.'

— *Anita Cleare, mother and author of* The Work/Parent Switch

'*How to Have Incredible Conversations with Your Child* stands out from any other parental book for its well thought out process to bring theory to practice. It's a treasure chest full of tools to get conversations started, but is also directed towards meaningful exchanges with your children. The language is accessible, even if the terms introduced are not simple, and one feels encouraged to try their approach after the first chapters. I found the use of visuals particularly useful – these are not only a brilliant tool for kids to communicate but also for parents to remember frameworks and use them when the right moment happens. I'd recommend this book to any parent who is looking for research-based, applicable ideas to connect with their children.'

— *Laia Collazos, mother of two girls*

'I'm a big fan of everything Jane and Bettina do, and this book is no exception. I love the authors' warm and encouraging advice for having better conversations and ultimately improving our relationships with our children. We put so much effort into improving our communication skills with our partners, friends and colleagues, but the authors have encouraged us to prioritise improving our conversations with the young people in our life. Good conversations with our children? What a gift for everyone involved!'

— *Courtney Adamo, mother of five and founder of @babyccinokids*

'This is the book that will tell you how to build the emotional health of your child and at the same time build the relationship between the two of you. It is practical, wise and fun. The authors draw upon their extensive experience as clinical child psychologists and their deep knowledge of the modern scientific study of child development. Woven into their practical guidance about how to have conversations with your child are memorable drawings and icons which help build your appreciation of what will be a satisfying and rewarding process.'

— *Peter Hill, professor and consultant in child and adolescent psychiatry*

'Some books offer wonderful advice, but struggle to provide activities that take into account the needs of those who learn differently. You do not have to worry here, the visual representations of the topics being discussed helped my son (who is autistic) to make sense of our conversations. The guidance provided made it very manageable and encouraged us to take small steps in our conversations – you may not complete the whole activity in one sitting, and that's okay. Not only does this book offer great conversation starters, it offers a space for you and your child to revisit a topic whenever the need arises...revisiting these activities, over time, will help me and my son to develop new skills. This is a great book and has lots to offer. If you are looking for a book that will help you to develop your child's self-awareness, while developing their resiliency in the process, this is the book for you!'

— Claire Prosser, mother of Seb and founder of Spectropolis

'I liked talking about my feelings. I love staying at my nan's house but don't like leaving. My mum told me that it was okay to feel sad about it. She helped me to find things that would make me feel better.'

— Seb has autism and is aged 9

'This is a wonderfully engaging book written by two experienced and passionate clinicians aimed at enriching and supporting conversations and relationship building between parent, carer and/ or supportive adults with their children. There are also a range of lovely interactive activities and doodles to make the information more accessible and creative; as well as some sample conversations to offer some tangible ideas and examples of implementing the ideas in real world conversations. A fantastic addition to any parent.'

— Dr Karen Treisman, clinical psychologist, trainer, organizational consultant and author of 12 books including the bestselling A Therapeutic Treasure Box for Working with Children and Adolescents with Developmental Trauma *(www.safehandsthinkingminds.co.uk)*

How to Have
Incredible
Conversations
with Your Child

by the same authors

The Incredible Teenage Brain
Everything You Need to Know to Unlock Your Teen's Potential
Bettina Hohnen, Jane Gilmour and Tara Murphy
Foreword by Sarah Jayne Blakemore
ISBN 978 1 78592 557 3
eISBN 978 1 78450 952 1

of related interest

Creative Ways to Help Children Manage BIG Feelings
A Therapist's Guide to Working with Preschool and Primary Children
Dr Fiona Zandt and Dr Suzanne Barrett
Foreword by Associate Professor Lesley Bretherton
ISBN 978 1 78592 074 5
eISBN 978 1 78450 487 8

Creative Ways to Help Children Manage Anxiety
Ideas and Activities for Working Therapeutically with
Worried Children and Their Families
Dr Fiona Zandt and Dr Suzanne Barrett
Foreword by Dr Karen Cassiday
ISBN 978 1 78775 094 4
eISBN 978 1 78775 095 1

CBT Doodling for Kids
50 Illustrated Handouts to Help Build Confidence and
Emotional Resilience in Children Aged 6–11
Tanja Sharpe
ISBN 978 1 78592 537 5
eISBN 978 1 78775 017 3

How to Have Incredible Conversations with Your Child

A book to use together. A place to make conversation. A way to build your relationship.

Jane Gilmour and Bettina Hohnen

Illustrations by Douglas Broadley

Jessica Kingsley Publishers
London and Philadelphia

First published in Great Britain in 2022 by Jessica Kingsley Publishers
An Hachette Company

1

The fonts, layout and overall design of this book have been prepared according to dyslexia-friendly
principles. At JKP we aim to make our books' content accessible to as many readers as possible.

A CIP catalogue record for this title is available from the British Library and the Library of Congress

ISBN 978 1 78775 640 3
eISBN 978 1 78775 641 0

Printed and bound in Great Britain by Bell & Bain Limited

Jessica Kingsley Publishers' policy is to use papers that are natural, renewable and recyclable
products and made from wood grown in sustainable forests. The logging and manufacturing
processes are expected to conform to the environmental regulations of the country of origin.

Jessica Kingsley Publishers
Carmelite House
50 Victoria Embankment
London EC4Y 0DZ

www.jkp.com

Contents

Compass Point 2: How Are You?

These conversations help you think about the full range of emotions – the good, the bad and the ugly. They introduce us to the idea of sharing difficult feelings as well as all the good stuff. Make this a safe, comfortable place to talk and bring it on.

How are you? Mood Mountain

Sometimes it's hard to describe how you feel. This is an easy way to describe where you are at today, without saying a word.

How are you? How Do You Wheel?

Naming feelings is an important part of sorting them out. It is a powerful tool, and this is a gentle conversation to start the feeling wheel turning.

How are you? Playing Detective

We all pick up emotions from each other using 'clues'. This conversation invites a discussion about how different family members express different emotions. It is very useful for kids who struggle with social communication.

How are you? Worry Pots

This is a chance for children to describe who tends to hold onto a worry in a family, using just pictures. It is brilliant stuff for children who find it hard to find the words.

How are you? Heads and Hearts – Step 1

This is all about figuring out the difference between thoughts and feelings. It is great practice for worriers.

How are you? Heads and Hearts – Step 2

This conversation introduces the idea that we can decide how we feel, because we can change what we think.

Compass Point 3: What Helps?

These conversations are all about sorting through the resources, tools and support that we have to hand (or could use) when times are tough. A chance to talk about challenging times and think about them in a different way.

What helps? Ups and Downs

This is a really simple conversation that is good for the 'all or nothing' thinkers. It helps us to hold on to the idea that some days are better than others, even if it's just by a smidge.

What helps? Really Rubbish

Talking about bad times we have had in life creates a bond between us. It also reminds us that we get through even really bad days – they will pass.

Pick 'n' Mix

Communication is a two-way process, so this is a chance to mix it up a bit. Pick any one of the conversations and swap roles so that, this time, parents share *their* thoughts and feelings, and children listen. This is a great way to develop empathy.

Last Word

Appendix 1: Example Conversations

Appendix 2: Conversation Pathways

Acknowledgements

Jane

This book is about relationships, so now I take the chance to reflect on some of mine.

Bettina, in between pondering what lockdown(s) meant to us, our families and the young people in the world, we wrote *that* book. What delightful irony that despite being such a gentle and generous soul, you are *utterly ruthless* when it comes to evaluating data. So, grateful though I am for your incisive intellectual contribution, it is the unique brand of friendship and sorting space you offer that I consider my greatest and most precious prize.

Douglas, my lovely 'difficult illustrator' husband, our creative meetings for this book were very much like my life with you: excellent fun and so often blown away by how very *clever* you are; 604 out of 10 for you, DJB.

Gigi and O, writing stirred poignant memories of your first school years, when you inspired the concept for this book. In these pages, we describe the rock star qualities of parenthood and there were many times during our young family life that your carefully considered announcements ('Mama, when I hold your hand, it's like the sun' and 'Mama, you are like a sparkly mermaid') really did make me feel like a rock star. You inspire me still, as you grow into phenomenal young adults.

Gilmours, thanks for the great big ball of love and support you all are, especially to Mum for understanding, before the science told us, the fundamental value of warm and open communication, and to Dad for illustrating how to embrace hard conversations with twinkly-eyed charm.

And Samantha G, my elegant and thoughtful friend, thank you for your eagle eyes and that faultless opinion of yours.

Bettina

Having the opportunity to write a book is a real honour. Having the opportunity to write a book with your best friend is a dream come true. Jane, your warmth, empathy and incredible ability to connect with children shines through on every page of this book. There is nothing more important in life than relationships (as the data confirm) and the building block for relationships is conversation. I'm lucky as I get to do that with you almost every day. I truly cherish our relationship. I hear many people say writing a book is a lonely, arduous and serious endeavour. I've never had so much fun. To quote Piglet from *Winnie the Pooh*, 'It's so much more friendly with two'.

I had to pinch myself while sitting in the 'illustrator' zoom calls. To see your genius in action, Douglas, as we giggled and stumbled through a set of random ideas of what we were trying to express, was a privilege. It was magical how you brought the ideas to life and told the story through your illustrations.

My greatest pleasures in life have been the incredible conversations I have had with friends, family and my children, Ella and Billy. It is a commonly held belief that children learn more from their parents than parents learn from their children. I'm not so sure. I have learnt so much from seeing how my children navigate the world. Sometimes it's the little people who have the clearest vision.

Martin, I would be sitting in the dark, both literally and metaphorically, if it wasn't for you. It's not only because you do know how to change a light bulb but also because you pick up the trail I leave behind me so I'm able to obsess, as I tend to do, about emotions and children's wellbeing.

Thank you to my lovely friends who walked round and round the heath with me, for your companionship, stories and listening ears.

Finally, thank you again to my mother who inspired my love for this field.

We would both like to thank...

Sam, Alfie, Peter, Elliot, Nina, Drummond, Sophie and Bea, Ian, Virginia, Margo, Laura, Imogen and Freddie – we are so grateful for your time, energy and invaluable feedback during the *Incredible Conversation* Beta launch.

And finally, Amy, our wonderful, razor-sharp editor who took a chance on our pitch and believed we could meet that deadline when we weren't quite so sure...

Preface

This is not a book exactly – it's **a place to have incredible conversations with your child**. Conversation builds relationships, and successful relationships predict good mental health, higher academic success, improved resilience, a higher income, better employment satisfaction, stronger physical health and greater longevity. *Incredible Conversations* equal incredible wellbeing.

> **You:** How was your day?
> **Your child:** Fine.

In our experience, as parents and carers you want to communicate meaningfully with your child, to find out what is going on in their life at home and school. Are they feeling okay? How are friendships going? The difficulty is that, despite the best of intentions, it can be a struggle to find a 'way in'. **How exactly do you make 'it' happen?** We answer the million-dollar question by steering you through carefully supported and structured conversational platforms that encourage connections and strengthen relationship bonds.

You and your child will experience the book *together*, which makes it unique. The idea was developed in the course of 20 years of clinical psychology practice. In our sessions, parents are usually invited to sit alongside their child while we get to know the young person. We use a variety of conversation tools, and parents invariably comment that they discover whole aspects of their child's world during this process. Our communication approach is **a game-changer for any family of a primary/elementary school-age child**, and can inspire meaningful change in a relationship, with long-lasting benefits.

The simple ideas create a communication *experience*, for parents and children together. They are designed to be repeated because relationships are not single events – they evolve, particularly where fast-developing children are concerned. By making these conversations habitual in family life, you are laying down the foundation of a strong relationship with your child so they develop skills that last a lifetime and *benefit* them for a lifetime. There is powerful evidence that **good relationships improve the quality of life across the life span**. But we are not here to convince you of that evidence, because that is not the point of this book. Nope. Our offer is to **provide an inviting space to have conversations**, so you and your child develop the very relationship skills which underlie emotional and physical wellbeing.

The drawings, graphic ideas, key questions and concrete examples are specifically designed for primary/elementary school-age children, capitalizing on their stage of development. While this is a collaboration that is respectful of young people's opinions, parents are the grown-ups in the relationship and with that comes responsibility. So, before you start talking, we **get you into the best mindset and give you practical tips** about providing the best setting, how to respond, when to talk, when to act and when to *just listen*.

Connection and relationship skills are the greatest gift you can give your child because, with that, you hand them the keys to lifelong wellbeing. Use this book together and unlock the power of *Incredible Conversations*.

How to Have Incredible Conversations

Relationship skills are central to wellbeing

The evidence is overwhelming: a strong relationship with your child benefits you and them, both now and in the future. **Good relationships are consistently linked to lifelong positive emotional and physical wellbeing.** So, in our view, helping your child to learn to communicate on an emotional level should be number one on your parental 'to do' list. The value of relationships is certainly not 'soft science'; indeed, there is a recent surge of neuroscientific and cutting-edge data underlining their importance. Get the ability to form relationships right at home, early on, and it forms a template for successful peer and romantic relationships in the future. It predicts academic success, job satisfaction and better physical health. There are oodles of data showing that healthy family relationships can actually improve wellbeing and act as a protective factor against life challenges and mental health difficulties. Prevention is better than cure, so these conversations are aimed at families in which there is no particular crisis or problem to fix but who want to prepare their children for life in the best way they can.

Learning to talk and listen are as important as what is being said

Having a profound conversation with your child is one the greatest privileges of parenting; the opportunity to learn about your child's thoughts and feelings, their hopes and fears – and to share yours – is an extraordinary experience. It may mean that you are sharing for sharing's sake, or it may mean that there is a dream or a worry that would benefit from adult support or needs to be acted upon. All three scenarios are equally important. But having a conversation has more value than the information shared in the moment, it also means you are **learning together the *process* of meaningful connection**. Brain science tells us that sharing and *listening* have many benefits – particularly in moments of distress.

Relationships need regular maintenance or they break down

If you keep in touch emotionally with your child, it means you form a connection that will be resilient when times get tough and forms protection against the impact of negative events. This book gives you a place to communicate and a practical way to build your relationship, so that you can **create a bond that will tolerate the stresses of life**. We can't draw on relationships unless we invest in them regularly. For many children in the care system who have had discontinuity in their relationships, this investment is even more important. We must nurture our connections so they can tolerate some tension and we stay connected in difficult times. When life throws a challenge at your family, a deeper level of communication is required than the usual functional exchanges (for example, 'Have you done your homework?') or instructions (for example, 'Hang your coat up') that tend to dominate busy family life. Imagine a significant life event like a bereavement. Without having established and *learnt* patterns of communication and trust, it's unlikely that your child would want – or *know how* – to share their feelings. Consider the exercises we describe here as communication training, forming a new habit, so that your relationship develops strength and resilience, which means you will continue to communicate with one another when the pressure is on.

This isn't a parenting book, or a children's workbook – it's a joint experience for you and your child

There are many marvellous books on the market aimed at helping parents develop their communication skills but these are designed for parents to read alone, and then apply in their family relationships. We know parents describe having read these sort of books who say they find it hard to apply the ideas *in the moment*. Similarly, there are creative books aimed at primary/elementary school-age children to help them develop emotional literacy (which is a valid and important goal) but they are offered as 'workbooks' to be completed by children in isolation. There is a danger that all the wonderful thoughts and feelings invested in these workbooks will be lost because there is no forum for sharing – and sharing is key to a good relationship.

Parents often ask us for a sort of step-by-step guide to family communication, and we do exactly that, page by page. Our book takes effective family communication theories a step further down the line of application, so that it's as if **we are 'in the room' with you**. Parents are the adults, so it is you as parents who must scaffold the conversation with children. So, in Part 1, we offer tips, ideas and tools that **help orientate you into the best mindset for conversation** and relationship building with your child. Then, in Part 2, you will find the conversations: a *joint experience* where you and your child will have *Incredible Conversations* together. We give you reassuring props on which you can both lean, and a **creative forum for exploring thoughts and feelings**, to encourage a more profound connection with one another.

How to use this book

We have spent many hours making this book simple but, as the saying goes, 'simple is not the same as easy'. Simple means that the essence of an idea is more exposed so that it is accessible.

By paring down the principles of good conversation skills, we increase the chances of meaningful conversations inhabiting your family life, day after day.

First, we would strongly encourage you to **use the series of conversations in this book regularly**, perhaps repeating them every few months or so, because it takes repetition to lay down the brain circuits for any new skill and it takes time to establish habits and to build trust. Most parents would agree that one of their most treasured family possessions is the paracetamol sitting in their bathroom cabinet. In every bottle there is a hefty dose of flavouring and this is because children are likely to need to take it many times in the early years, therefore, it can't taste too awful. (Remember that song about a spoonful of sugar? It helps the medicine go down.) There is a similar principle with any regular family activity and conversation; in our case, if your child's experience of expressing themselves is aversive, they won't want to do it again. So, make like the strawberry flavouring and **foster a positive experience** so you motivate a lifelong habit of appropriate emotional expression.

Second, we suggest that you **do the exercises in the good times and the bad** – when things are settled at home as well as during the challenging periods. That way you can help your child recognize that our thoughts and feelings change over time and that life has light and shade. They can remember what helped before and recognize that they are developing new skills or ideas.

Third, we recommend that **both parents try these conversations** with children. Children often gravitate towards one specific parent for a particular need. The literature tells us the 'job' of dealing with emotions often falls to the main caregiver, which is, in many instances, Mum. In same-sex partnerships, too, roles are often divided in terms of different family responsibilities. We also know that children pick up a story about what's expected of them by watching their parents. Is the story in your house that the main wage earner doesn't 'do' emotion? If it is, what message does that send?

You are likely to be the CEO of feelings in your house because you are the one reading this book. If you have a partner and they wouldn't normally take part in the family's emotional discussions, we would encourage *them* to try these activities. Similarly, if you live separately from your child's other parent, send them a copy. The book is structured so that it is accessible, even if talking isn't in your comfort zone. You will be sending a powerful, positive message to your child if both parents take an active role in emotional wellbeing.

Remember to let your child lead, too. Let them control the agenda sometimes. In so much of family life the parent is in charge, but research shows that parents' relationships with their child are strengthened by 'horizontal' exchanges such as playing or drawing together, where respecting each other and enjoying each other are the main aims. This book is a place to do just that.

Four points on the wellbeing compass
We have developed four conversation topics on something we have called the 'wellbeing compass': they each have a section in Part 2, which includes a series of conversations for you to work through with your child. The four compass points are:

1. Who are you?
2. How are you?
3. What helps?
4. What gets in your way?

Each of these compass points has several different conversations and activities that accompany it. You can go through these in sequence, conversation by conversation, topic by topic, and we have ordered them with that in mind. However, you don't have to work through the conversations in this book from beginning to end. One conversation might take a few moments, others might last half an hour, so you certainly wouldn't go through all the conversations from start to finish in one go. Just **do as much or as little as your time and energy allow**.

At the end of the book we have also suggested several 'fast-track' **conversation pathways**, which are edited highlights tailored for different circumstances or different emotional or communication styles your child might use. However, you may dip into a particular topic or a single conversation in any order, or perhaps you will find one or two that are particularly useful and use them often.

Any and all of these approaches are valuable and will be useful depending on your need and motivation. Given that we suggest you repeat the same exercises throughout the pre-teen years, you might also **spend time together comparing or discussing previous conversations**.

Having the opportunity to look over your child's heartfelt drawings, thoughts or ideas from perhaps several years ago is a wonderful added bonus. *And* they are stored in one handy volume. You. Are. Welcome.

Who are you?

This might sound like an odd question for a parent to ask of their child, but the trick here is to be *genuinely* curious and leave your expectations to one side. If you take a position of authentic interest, it encourages all sorts of interesting responses. This insight into your child's inner world is valuable because if you know what really motivates your child (and not what they think you want to hear), then you will be better armed to help them navigate the inevitable bumps lying on their road ahead. By describing ourselves to others, we are also getting to know ourselves – a conversation is a sort of sorting space. There is a wave of new evidence showing that developing self-awareness early on in childhood is central to wellbeing.

How are you?

This section introduces the concept of feelings, explores the range of emotion in your child's repertoire and normalizes the idea of sharing positive and negative emotions with trusted people. Simply asking questions about a range of feelings means your child will develop greater self-awareness, which takes time to learn.

What helps?

We all have ways of coping. Sometimes we are not aware of our responses; at other times we consciously develop coping strategies. This section helps you discover and catalogue your child's coping skills and support systems, which in itself is empowering.

What gets in your way?
We all have moments where we trip up or make choices that might inhibit development and growth. The first step in shaking off these unhelpful responses is to be aware of them. This section helps children notice what gets in the way of making positive choices.

Pick 'n' mix

Here you can invite your child to **pick one or two of the conversations** that catch their eye, but this time *they* 'host' the conversation, asking you the questions – you swap roles. Mixing it up like this, with *you* sharing your thoughts and feelings, is highly engaging for a young child and an opportunity to share from your perspective. You might also turn to this section if your child is getting stuck in other conversations. It means you can model some great relationship skills to your child and show them how to listen and share – after all, we are hoping to encourage and learn two-way conversation skills.

An accessible layout designed for you both

Each conversation idea in Part 2 is presented over four pages and is a shared place for you both to have your conversation together.

On the first page there is a brief summary of the idea behind each conversation. The wording is very straightforward and we address both parents and children so you can read it together. What better way to start sharing relationship ideas? However, many children (particularly younger ones) won't be interested in the preamble at all and that's okay – it doesn't fundamentally change the experience. The double page spread is where the conversation really happens. On the **left-hand page** there are conversation starters and ideas for you to extend the discussion. Use these phrases just as they are or adapt them in any way that is useful. On the **right-hand page** you will find a page for you and your child to complete together, where ideas are presented in an engaging, concrete and visual way so that children can relate to them. They can hang their own ideas on the visuals to express themselves, and you can discuss together their drawings, pictures, colours or words and co-create an *Incredible Conversation*.

Finally, there is a page to reflect on the conversation you have just had. This is designed mainly for parents to use and to perhaps make some notes about the conversation. In some cases, children may want to join this activity, so there is a space for them to do that if they want (for example, they might rate the conversation out of 10). However, most children will be ready for a break. Don't force it if they have had enough.

You can download the conversations, so you have multiple copies available, from www.jkp.com/catalogue/book/9781787756403

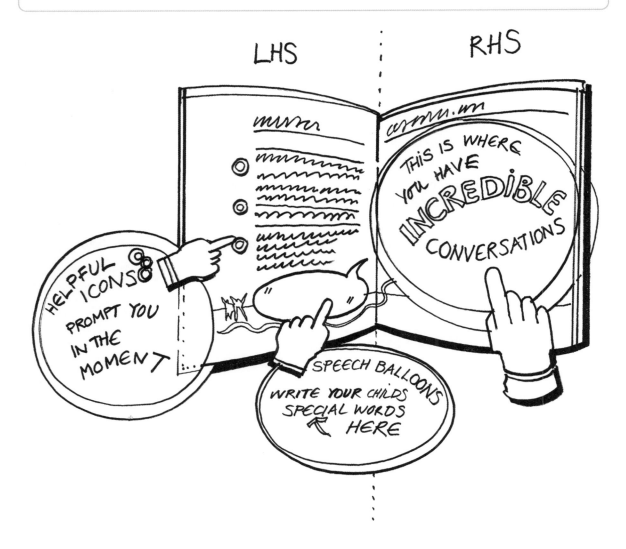

You will find **example conversations** at the end of the book, which might give you some inspiration (these are real by the way, and reproduced with kind permission). Your conversation drawings will look different to the examples, of course, but it might help you get started. You'll also see little **bite-sized 'signposts'** in each conversation to prime you, remind you of the best communication mindset and keep you going.

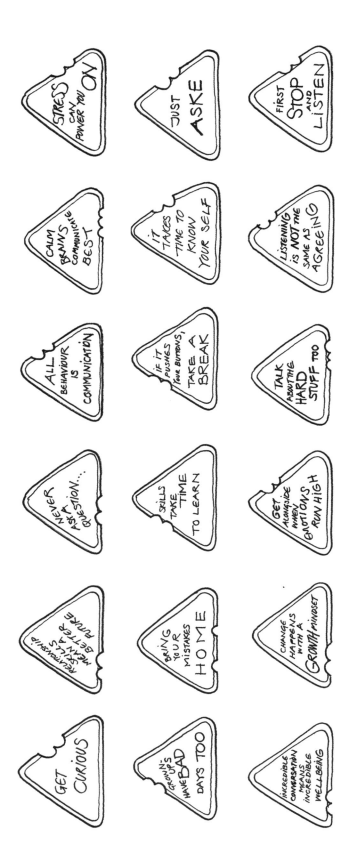

The bite-sized signposts

There are **speech balloons** on the conversation pages so you can note your child's important words or phrases (you can include a date if you like that sort of thing). If you can, write them down word for word because there is nothing quite so empowering for a child as an adult noting down *exactly* what they have said. This might sound like a minor point, but what it stands for is important – when adults take an approach like this, it validates children's ideas and that has strong links with positive wellbeing for children.

Make our terminology work for you

We use terminology in the broadest sense and encourage you to do that too. For example, 'family' might mean the people that live together in your house, but they may live in separate households; similarly, 'family members' might be related to each other or might not. Relationships matter – at home, at school on the sports field and at work. So, although we use the term 'parents' throughout, we know that adults looking after children in different areas of life (for example, teachers, social workers, mentors or even sports coaches) will find these ideas useful.

Any adult who has a meaningful relationship with a child could use the book with 'their' children. And while we are on the subject of demographics, although these conversation platforms have been developed with children aged up to about 12 years old in mind, tweens and teenagers may continue to relate to the concepts well into adolescence. If it works for you, then it works for us.

An important disclaimer: many of these ideas are influenced by a variety of therapeutic schools and evidence-based techniques. If we listed each piece of theory individually each time it was relevant, it would make the book too cumbersome. Instead, we have included a 'Further Reading' list at the end of the book, in case you are interested in finding out more about the conversation activities underpinnings in current psychological theory. Some conversation ideas appear so simple, you might consider them simplistic – but don't be fooled. The trick here is not the question so much as thinking about the delivery – each micro-moment of your time together and the *experience* of talking together. The art of conversation, indeed.

The icons

If you've read our previous book, *The Incredible Teenage Brain* (see 'Further Reading'), you will know how much we like an icon, because they help you navigate the book easily so you maximize your time. In a world knee-deep in emojis and emoticons, we can all relate to them. We use them here and there in Part 1, 'Your Communication Mindset', but most often you will see them in Part 2, 'The Incredible Conversations', where they appear in the conversation activities to prompt you in the moment.

Information
We have included a few words on the **scientific evidence**, describing the significance of the topic in terms of psychological wellbeing. It's very brief, but enough to validate your efforts.

Growing up
This icon highlights aspects of your child's development that are likely to **change during the primary/ elementary school years**.

Anything goes
This icon acts as a reminder that there are **no right or wrong answers when it comes to how you feel**. It is a great compliment to be in anyone's confidence, so make sure your child gets that sense from you. It's sometimes hard to hear about difficulties in your child's life, but we want your child to feel confident that they can tell you anything. Give them the message that what is true for them, is okay to tell you. Notice that this is *not* the same as agreeing with it. The message is more: tell me about it; we can figure this out together so you can move on. Some parents worry that by showing understanding of how their child sees a situation they are somehow agreeing with it, accepting bad behaviour, or that it will make the feeling worse. The opposite is true. Listening and accepting helps a child make sense of their experiences.

Sshh
You might find this icon counterintuitive in a book about conversation, but it is a place-keeper for **keeping quiet**. You can telegraph care and support by staying alongside your child in the same room, without saying anything at all. It often means that your child finds the thinking space to say a little more, and sort it through by themselves.

Conversation starters
Here, we give some **phrases that you can use** to introduce the idea. It's a guide rather than a script, and you may prefer to paraphrase it or tailor it specifically so it feels right for you both. The **keep talking** section includes ways to extend the discussion.

End positively
It is very important that you end with **appreciation and praise**, whether the discussion went wrong, it included difficult feelings or your child declined, appropriately, to talk. This will also ensure your child keeps coming back to you, in the good times and the bad (remember the 'spoonful of sugar' principle). Having an ending ritual really makes it feel like the conversation counts. We've used a fist bump, but better still, make up your own. It means you can end and celebrate it together.

Boom! You've just had an *Incredible Conversation*.

You'll become very familiar with these icons as they appear throughout the book, but here is an easy way to remember the key points: just **ASKE**:

Anything goes
Shh (sometimes)
Keep talking
End positively

The *Incredible Conversations* Mission Statement

This is more than a book. This is an experience you create together with your child. It is a *joint invitation* to participate in the reciprocal, authentic communication that forms the bedrock of healthy relationships and, with it, lifelong wellbeing. Children do not develop their communication skills in a vacuum or in the abstract – younger and pre-teenage children in particular need to *experience* ideas to absorb them effectively. If you take the time to explore the conversation platforms in this book together, you will find that meaningful connections, emotional literacy and secure relationships are the precious products of these *Incredible Conversations*.

PART 1

Your Communication Mindset

Ideas and tips for parents to hold in mind to unlock
the best conversation experience with children

Chapter 1

Relationships and Communication Skills – Why They Matter

Good relationships predict a better future

The evidence is vast, so we've made a long story, short

Learning how to form a healthy relationship is very much worthwhile, for so many reasons. In this chapter we provide a rundown of why, and how science shows us that this really does matter.

As parents ourselves, we haven't forgotten how wonderful but utterly exhausting young family life can be. Addressing your children's physical needs sometimes means that it's very hard to find space to address their emotional health (or indeed yours).

For that reason, we have made this book and the conversations in it extremely simple and immediately accessible.

At the same time, **we believe strongly in an evidence-based practice**. While there is a wealth of strong scientific data and many years of clinical practice behind the concepts we use in this book, we have taken a decision not to go into too much depth presenting the evidence. Rest assured, however, that the evidence most certainly exists.

In our experience, many parents are enormously well informed about developmental theories and psychological principles, so we invite this section of our readership (you know who you are) to look at the 'Further Reading' list at the end of the book.

Whatever your views, and whatever your exhaustion or knowledge level, we outline below the key themes from the scientific literature.

If you feel disheartened, or when things seem to go pear-shaped once again, come back to this chapter and read through the headings. It will refuel your efforts and remind you why relationships matter – very much.

Every genuine connection attempt counts, no matter how your child responds in that moment

There will be times when you attempt to connect with your child and it might be hard or upsetting; it might possibly feel unfulfilling or even pointless. We guarantee it won't be warm and fuzzy every time you use this book, but as we strive to reflect real-world relationships, that is to be expected.

Our hope is that you and your child get through a tricky conversation and stay connected, because that is the essence of a good relationship.

Every warm and genuine attempt on your part to connect with your child *matters* to your relationship and to your child. Your child may not respond, appear not to have heard, or push you away emotionally or physically, but your overtures mean that they will be marinated in loving communication.

Every time you down tools to listen to something that is important to your child, it matters and it will be filed away and stored in their 'how to form a relationship' database. Further, you will be teaching them, implicitly, some superb communication skills. Each time you make that investment, you are giving your child the message that you want to hear about their world and that their thoughts and ideas matter to you.

Small actions now have a major impact in the future

Does the flap of a butterfly wing in Brazil cause a tornado in Texas? More than 50 years ago, mathematician Edward Norton Lorenz theorized that minor events have a significant influence on the world further down the line. Though originally a weather theory, this question has been used as a metaphor in many different contexts. In human relationships, the short answer is yes, it does. Apparently inconsequential moments that you grab with your child are actually the means by which you change the course of your young person's life trajectory. The most powerful interventions are often nothing fancy or complicated, but what makes them life-changing is that they fit into our everyday life, and so we are more likely to do that good stuff over and over again.

Every time you offer a warm, consistent, open dialogue, consider it an intervention. These little events add up to have a major, long-lasting impact on your child. The key is to embed connection into your everyday routine. Here is a perfect example (with strong evidence to support it): families who regularly have dinner together have children who do better in terms of mental health and academic performance. At every mealtime these children are learning and shaping their relationship with the family.

A good parent–child relationship means your child is likely to be satisfied with life

Positive relationships actively *change* a child's wellbeing for the better. This is not to say that other factors don't influence wellbeing, but parent–child relationships are a fundamental part of the picture. Think about this for a moment. There is so much in our world we can't predict or control (COVID-19 certainly taught us that), but the communication style you have with your child is within your sphere of influence and is an opportunity to improve your child's wellbeing. *You* can set the tone for the relationship that you have with your child.

Positive parent–child communication is linked to better future adult relationships

As young children become young adults, their life satisfaction is more influenced by the quality of peer relationships. Peers are everything to them because they represent their future community and they need to figure out how to be part of that group. Even so, parent–child relationships continue to be the bedrock for future relationships in adolescence.

Evidence shows that young people who grow up in a family who can talk about their shared experiences (especially the challenging times) have better mental health. In addition, a close relationship with parents in childhood predicts 'happiness' in adulthood. The most likely explanation for this is that healthy family communication is the training ground for positive future relationships. Young children learn their first communication patterns in their family, and they take these approaches and apply them to peers, adult friends and romantic partners, and even work colleagues. If you get this skill going in the family setting, your child will develop a superpower for forming relationships wherever they go in life.

A few moments of warmth with your child have a positive impact

If your relationship isn't quite as close as you'd like, that's okay. All relationships go through ebbs and flows, but as the grown-up in the relationship, it's up to you to make the changes for the better. If you make overtures and are patient and consistent, in time you will develop a more meaningful connection with your child. Ideally, we want family life to be calm because conflict can have long-lasting effects on children and their brains. However, we know that calm may not always reign. Even if (possibly, particularly if) there is significant conflict around a young person, or your relationship with one another is volatile, a daily dose of warmth and positivity from you has a powerful healing effect. You may not be able to control conflict in your house for a variety of reasons but you can guarantee warm moments with your child.

Positive relationships are linked to physical and mental health and academic achievement

Actually, as far as we are concerned, emotional wellbeing is the *only* outcome that matters. But we are psychologists, so we would say that wouldn't we?

Here is the bottom line: human beings need connection; and if we can't maintain fulfilling relationships, then there are serious repercussions for us in a whole range of domains. Studies that follow people from birth to old age provide very convincing evidence on the importance of relationships throughout the life span. Put simply, good relationships provide a wellbeing buffer against potential mental health disorders. (Incidentally, if you have a child on the autism spectrum, the picture is slightly different, though these young people still have a need for connection. For more on this, see 'Children with social communication difficulties will respond well to these conversation ideas' in Chapter 3.) From these studies, we can confidently say that relationship building is the single most important capacity in the human condition: it predicts better exam performance, greater academic success, a higher income, better employment satisfaction, more fulfilling relationships with work and better physical health. The capacity to build relationships means a longer, healthier and more fulfilled life, whichever way you look at it.

Chapter 2

Relationships and Communication Skills – It's a Work in Progress

We learn relationship and communication skills over time and in different ways

Conversation and relationship building takes time to learn, just like any skill

The first time you do anything probably won't be your best attempt, because 'learning' means we need to allow the neurons in our brain to make links and develop circuits. With time, our brain circuits get stronger as we repeat the behaviour. The more we do something – so long as our strategy is good – the better we will get at it. There are special networks in the brain for forming and keeping relationships (which tells us how important evolution sees them for the survival of the species), but they have to be used if they are to develop. This means we need practice by discussing, thinking and connecting with others, so we get to know ourselves, understand our emotions and learn how to manage conflict.

Children learn by watching

Richard Davidson, an expert in how the brain understands emotions, argues that we should see compassion in the same way as learning language: our brain is primed to learn both these skills but will only learn them if they are modelled by those around us. One of the most powerful ways that children learn is by watching what you do, what matters to you, and even how you treat yourself. Ron Dahl, a US Paediatrician and Developmental Scientist, described a story to us which illustrates this point beautifully: young apprentice Buddhist monks get into fierce competition to show kindness to one another because it is considered so valuable by the adult priests around them. By the same token, how you react, even when (perhaps especially when) you are caught off-guard in unplanned moments of family life, matters. Telling your child to 'do as I say, not what I do' is pretty pointless. This is not an attempt to make you feel overwhelmed – no one can get it right all the time – but it's important to practise what you preach. ***Model* relationship skills to your children. Using this book together with your child, is one very effective way of doing that.**

We all respond to attention from others

As human beings, we are tuned into attention from others – we are *all* 'attention seekers' if you like. It's what makes us social beings and it means that the reaction of others to our behaviour influences the chances of it happening again. This is particularly true for children, who are very tuned into their parents' actions. Anything that gets a reaction from you (good or bad) is more likely to happen again. The most efficient way to increase the frequency of behaviour in your children is to praise it, discuss it and applaud it (but negative attention such as rows, telling off or scolding count as attention too). By the same token, anything that is consistently ignored by you is more likely to disappear. So, look out for any well-intentioned attempts at connection or relationship building and let your child know how delighted you are to see it.

Yes, please make mistakes, but do it the smart way and use a growth mindset

We all make mistakes, but the way you manage them is crucial to children's learning experience. We strongly recommend using a 'growth mindset', which means you believe you can become accomplished at pretty much anything or change something by using a good strategy and repeating it over and over again. A growth mindset means that mistakes are considered information to help us improve, finesse our strategy and move forward. Becoming an artist doesn't just happen; it comes from practice and persistence. If you model this idea from day to day, you will be teaching your child important life skills that will change the outcome in schoolwork, friendships and many other aspects of life. Don't get us started on the multitude of ways we can teach young people – it's one of our favourite topics and we could go on *and on*... In fact, we describe the opportunities and challenges in young people's learning in our previous book, *The Incredible Teenage Brain* (see 'Further Reading'), so if you want to know more about the learning process, look it up there.

Rupture and repair

It is normal for tensions to exist in any relationship. Therapists often refer to these tensions as 'ruptures'. They might be minor (for example, being a bit abrupt towards someone) or more serious (for example, getting angry and losing control). Repair can be an apology (for example, 'I really upset you yesterday'), being able to accept an apology (for example, 'I know you didn't mean to hurt me') or can just be an acknowledgement that you are willing to listen. Philippa Perry describes the importance of this process superbly in *The Book You Wish Your Parents Had Read* (see 'Further Reading'). It is important for children to learn (and experience) that rupture can be followed by repair, as part of their relationship-building skills. You can help them learn this by watching out for any repair bids, however tiny, and meet them half way by accepting them. Surviving ruptures, and making the repair, can actually make the relationship stronger, just like the darned toe in a sock. The darned part is likely to be the strongest part and can tolerate more wear than the parts that have not been repaired.

Look back at past conversations and talk about how things were then

So, give yourself a break, and expect some false starts as you both learn to move your relationship along. Just keep going and have another go when the time is right. These repetitions are not only about developing your skills, they have another benefit. Some of your conversations might take place during a calm phase of family life, and others when things are tough, but it all makes up life's rich tapestry. In addition, looking back at a difficult period and talking through how you both figured it out highlights the skills you have learnt, lays the foundations for recovery, and so builds a self-belief in resilience for the next challenge on the horizon.

Capitalizing on the characteristics of middle childhood to learn communication skills

Primary/elementary school-age children are primed to learn from you, to be around you

For pre-adolescent children, parents are veritable rock stars (trust us, it's true). This is not to say your relationship will always be positive, but parents do sometimes forget how central they are to their child's world view. Spending *time* with you is more valuable than any material thing, expensive holiday or amount of screen time. Primary/elementary school children are highly motivated to be around you and will likely consider a joint activity a positive experience and a real treat. The one-to-one attention will be extremely rewarding for you both. With the onset of puberty, young people are drawn towards their peers and independence, which can change the tone of family life, and with it you will need to adjust your parenting approach. Although adolescents are separating from you in preparation for adulthood, they still need nurturing adult relationships to help them navigate the world (despite what they may tell their parents in the heat of the moment). Taking time to learn relationship and conversation skills together with your primary/elementary school-age child is far-sighted because you can draw on this investment when teenage issues present. Parents of teenagers will say that the challenges of adolescence require an open line of communication between you and your teen. You want them to share and problem solve with you, and that can only happen from a solid, trusting foundation.

Using visual material is perfect for helping primary/ elementary school-age children communicate

With middle childhood in mind, the conversation props are developed specifically for this stage of cognitive development. We know that younger children respond best to concrete things (for example, a drawing or a model) rather than abstract concepts or ideas. We use a variety of visual analogies to give children a platform to describe how they are feeling, using something real as a conduit for their expression. It is also (dare we say it?) rather less boring than just using words, if you are under 12 years old. As clinical psychologists, we wouldn't attempt a therapy session with this age group without drawing materials. You will learn as you go, how you can change the focus of the conversation by turning to a new page, lift the energy by swapping colours, or imply the shared partnership of your communication by taking turns to make marks on the page. This latter point is important. If you like your drawings very neat, be prepared to put a lid on any urges to correct your child's drawings. Resist correcting spelling or letter formation – that's something for schoolwork and doesn't belong in our *Incredible Conversations* – otherwise, we might be conveying the message that the feeling your child is writing or drawing isn't 'right'. This is very different from accepting any behaviour, of course. All feelings are acceptable, and learning to *express* them in a shared and pro-social way is our goal. Feeling angry is perfectly valid, but we have to learn how to express our anger appropriately.

Children will love to talk about their younger selves with you

There are other benefits to making this scrapbook of conversations together during childhood, because looking together at the ideas you recorded in the past is a bonding experience in and of itself. We know from the mental health literature that discussing this sort of material with each other will have a variety of positive effects on the parent–child relationship and general wellbeing. It's a precious opportunity to stop and think about each other. All children enjoy reminiscing about their past selves with a loved one, but children who have experienced discontinuity and uncertainty in relationships will particularly benefit from this type of communication. Your child will gain so much from looking at the development of their past selves, seeing in real terms that they have learnt new skills, can describe different feelings and have got through tricky periods.

Chapter 3

Top Tips

Practical tips so your conversation goes well

Plan your *Incredible Conversations* to increase your odds of success

Have a think about your setting before you start the conversation. You know your child, so avoid any trigger points that have been wind-ups in the past. This will likely mean that you select a time when you are *both* unhurried, well fed and well rested, and there are as few distractions as possible. If you have a quiet child, they may need some time after a school day to decompress, so let them have some space, perhaps alone if that's their preference, before you try to talk. It's ideal to do these exercises one-on-one, rather than with the whole family, because younger children may be tempted to copy older siblings, and so on. If you have other kids of an appropriate age, use these conversations with them too. It's important to convey parity and offer that one-to-one golden time with all the children at home rather than singling out one child. This cover-all approach will also mean you are less likely to be disturbed, as everyone knows their time will come.

Calm brains communicate best

As a parent, it is likely that there will be times when you feel really anxious about your child – it can be exhausting caring so deeply for another person's wellbeing. And these are the very times that you may want to have one of the conversations in this book. This is a good idea, of course; but at the same time, be aware that when you are feeling very stressed, you may become a little more intense or rigid (or whatever effect anxiety has on you), which will influence your communication style. So, take a breath and try to act low-key, practically breezy, even if you are not feeling it. If you are emitting anxiety, your child's brain is getting a message that their world is a dangerous place and so it may move into survival mode. As far as our brains are concerned, surviving is priority and thinking is a luxury. If the brain senses danger, it puts all its energy into the bits of the brain that make sure we survive. It won't have any spare resources for the 'thinking parts' of the brain where we solve problems and consider ideas carefully. When we think that the world is safe, *then and only then* will our brain allow energy into its thinking areas. This means that children in a calm state may be able to reflect on themselves a little, make connections, and so on. If you telegraph calm, your child will be able to engage with you and share meaningful thoughts, feelings and ideas.

You can say a lot by saying nothing at all

Let's say your child is having a tough time at school. Maybe they are being bullied, and you may well have paced the floor wondering how their day is going. It is very hard to resist pouncing on your child as soon as they come home from school, asking how the day went, but resist it you must. Allowing your child some time to process their day may mean that the conversation you have is a more meaningful one. You can still communicate caring as soon as you meet without any words and without firing questions at your child. A hug or a look can emit a deep level of caring and empathy. In fact, many brain science studies have shown that just having a loved one in the same room, saying *nothing whatsoever* decreases distress and anxiety in a profound way. Being alongside in this way, saying little, while emotions are intense, is all part of your communication toolkit. The time for talking will come, but choose it when you are *both* settled and ready.

Read the room: pick up your child's signals, and respond to them

Being able to respond to the messages that your child is sending out in their words or actions is one of the *most* important skills in good parent–child relationship building. We know that parents who can show that sort of sensitivity are more likely to have strong and secure relationship with their children. But it is quite a challenge to describe what this means in practical terms because it is so situation-specific. It covers a multitude of relationship skills such as reflecting and describing your child's state to your child and a response to the way they feel. For example, parents of infants might say, 'That's a big yawn. I think you are tired. Let's turn the lights off.' This is how very young children start to understand themselves. This skill can, and should, be meaningfully applied well into adolescence, though of course the issues are more complex and they need to be delivered in a way that is age-appropriate. 'Reading' your child may mean saying nothing, it may mean repeating back what you child has said, it may mean drawing a warm but firm boundary, it may even mean taking a step back; but what it certainly means is that you are watching and reading your child's state, considering it and using it to inform your next communication move, whether that is a word, a look, a touch or a pause. You can see how these parent–child moments translate into other relationships into adulthood. It takes reading the room to a whole new level.

A reluctant participant? Any bad associations with a paper and pen?

Although in our experience many children are positively raring to go if their parent invites them to do pretty much anything together, for other children, sitting down with a parent with a paper and pen in orbit might raise some strong negative associations with homework experiences. Our brains are wired to find patterns and links and that means if a pen and paper have been linked to stressful times in the past for a child, their brain will move into siege mode at the mere sight of the pen. If your child struggles with written tasks or feels stressed at the thought of homework, your job is to make this conversation experience as different as possible from homework. For some parents, homework sessions are described as 'battles'. Our aim in this book is to *draw* you together (get it?).

This is not homework, so don't make it feel like it is

So, your task is to deliver a non-homework feel. It may mean trying a different setting (outside if the weather is good, lying on the floor if it's not, and so on). Invite novelty if that keeps the conversation going. For example: you might ask active or younger children to do a lap of the room now and again or to talk while they are standing on their head (we can personally recommend headstand discussions); you might invite favourite toys or the dog to take part. Try anything that keeps your child's interest. In other words, there is no need to sit still, quietly, write neatly or spell correctly when it comes to these exchanges. If you can, invest in some totally epic coloured pens that would never be used for homework, not least because colour is such a useful way of communicating. However, none of these tips is as important as this **single most important point: shake off *your* feeling that this is a task that has to be 'done'**. Instead, if you radiate the idea that you are genuinely curious about what your child has to say – whatever they say – then you are much more likely to have an eager participant and a positive atmosphere.

It takes time to learn new habits, especially if the old routines were stressful

If talking isn't their thing, your child has trouble focusing, or you are working to shake off previous negative experiences, you will need to adjust your expectations accordingly. In other words, you may get everything 'right' in terms of delivery, atmosphere and setting, but your child may still be reticent to engage. This is understandable and it takes time to 'unlearn' habits, especially if they have been learnt in emotional circumstances. If your child is extremely upset or resistant then *that* itself is a communication (repeat after us...'all behaviour is communication'). Remember you are modelling communication skills, so try not to indicate that you feel irritation or disappointment; instead, voice the idea that you have got the message that your child doesn't want to join in and then wonder out loud why. The key with reluctant kids is to start slowly and aim to do only a few minutes together, then quit while you are ahead before frustration, anxiety or boredom set in. Maybe you get as far as choosing the conversation for the next time. You can call that a resounding success (because it is). Make sure your child knows how proud you are of them for taking a chance on trying it with you, especially if they eyed the idea with suspicion at first. You have started to teach them that talking is okay and that you are interested in their ideas, whatever they are. In time, you may be able to have slightly longer conversations or perhaps you may not need to deliver the setting so carefully. It will take some effort on your part, but it will be well worth it (have a quick re-read of 'Good relationships predict a better future' in Chapter 1). It also means you are showing that by using lived experience you can work through difficult things together and change them.

Is your child resistant or avoidant? The reasons may not be what you first assume...

If you have a child that is resistant to homework or to brushing their teeth or to anything really, there is likely to be a reason and we just need to figure out what it is. Hold on, though... It's not quite as simple as that because as parents we often make assumptions and we have to leave these at the door and be genuinely curious. This position of true curiosity will take the negative tone out of exchanges. Asking the question rhetorically, and perhaps in frustration: 'Why on earth, don't you just do your teeth?' is very different to 'I can see you don't like doing your teeth. I wonder why?' You just never know what you are going to hear. After 20-plus years of clinical practice and family life, we are still amazed by the answers we get when our question is really authentic. In some cases, the barriers your child describes may be eminently fixable, but unless we know, we can't fix them. In other cases, there is nothing to be fixed exactly, but sharing what is so fundamentally terrible about teeth brushing can be a test-run for other tricky issues, so *do not underestimate its importance*. Even if there is nothing that can be done about teeth brushing, your child has learnt that they can speak up about things that are troublesome and you will take it on board. You might 'just' empathize and agree it's a bit dull, but the process of empathizing is relationship gold dust (with bucket loads of brain science to back this up). Picture your family a few years from now: you have a teenager who is struggling with coursework, friendships or the expectations at a party, but so much of a teenager's life happens when parents aren't around. Our goal here is to bring up a teenager who has learnt that they won't be told off if they raise their struggles with you, that they can bring their problems home without fear of judgement. This gives you a chance to help your children problem solve and generalize learning principles from mistakes so that they make positive choices in the future. You won't ever pass up a chance to talk about teeth brushing again, will you?

Look after spontaneous communications – they are valuable

So, communication is everywhere if you just know how to translate it. Some parents describe a related issue and notice that their children tend to pipe up with a head-turning thought, idea or worry when it is least expected. Take these spontaneous moments and catch them with both hands, because you want to give your child the message that you are keen to hear whatever nugget they offer. If you can, stop what you are doing, switch off your phone, sit down and listen. If these episodes tend to happen when you are on your way out the door or about to drop your child off at school, it probably isn't a coincidence as these cliffhanger comments often come when children are about to separate from their trusted adult. If that's the case, let them know you have heard, make a promise you can keep about coming back to it (and stick to it), then ask to hear more when you can take the time to listen.

What pushes your buttons?

Parents are only human and have vulnerabilities like everyone else, but since we are the grown-ups we take the greatest share of responsibility and may have to overcome our own challenges as part of our duty of care. One key communication tip is to be aware of what pushes your buttons in a conversation. You may find it hard to see your child feeling angry, or maybe avoidance is what really winds you up. Children will sense your response when they express whatever pushes your buttons, and may take from it the idea that it is shameful (for example) to feel that way. It is likely to take a supreme effort on your part to manage your response, and there may be complex reasons why these emotions or approaches to life are hard to be around for you (often it's a trigger from a previous experience or relationship). Try to talk it through with a partner or friend to take the 'heat out of it' and help you tolerate these moments with your child.

Children with social communication difficulties will respond well to these conversation ideas

We've established that relationship building is a work in progress, whatever our age and circumstances, and at the same time, some aspects of our profile and our child's profile will impact on their conversation skills. The most obvious example concerns the autism spectrum. Autistic children may find it hard to describe their own emotions or understand other people's thoughts and feelings. Children on the autism spectrum may well be articulate and talkative but they may find the to and fro of communication a challenge. Classically, children with social communication difficulties are motivated to connect but find having a conversation (just in and of itself) so challenging that they miss out on the chance to develop their emotional literacy in that conversation 'sorting space'. It's a double whammy, if you like. A visual expression of the ideas being discussed can be helpful to support these young people in conversation; similarly, a clear structure helps them figure out the expectations in a social situation. The *Incredible Conversations* in Part 2 deliver this type of scaffolding.

Neurodiversity and executive function difficulties influence conversation skills

There are many other aspects of neurodiversity that impact on communication. Young people with attention deficit hyperactivity disorder (ADHD) have problems with turn taking and might find the unstructured nature of conversation difficult. Dyslexic children may have trouble with their working memory (a sort of holding room for information), which is crucial for conversation skills, and they may have language processing difficulties that make it hard to follow information that is only presented orally. In fact, it is true to say that almost all neurodiverse conditions involve the 'executive functions' (a term that describes cognitive abilities such as flexibility, organization and emotional regulation). If your child has a neurodiverse condition or even very mild executive function difficulties, these may well have an impact on their conversation skills to a greater or lesser degree. The skills will still build, but it may be a slower process. Whether the issue is working memory, turn taking, difficulty focusing or problems articulating emotion, our conversation spaces will help with many of these vulnerabilities. For example, if you've lost your place in what you are saying, having a visual reminder in front of you acts as a place keeper. If it's hard to remember to pause and let your partner speak, use a 'chat hat' – whoever is wearing the hat, is allowed to speak (see 'What gets in the way? Muddle and Makeup' in Part 2).

Did the neurodiverse apple fall far from the tree ?

Neurodiversity often runs in families. If your child has ADHD, you or their other parent may well have these traits too. Similarly, if you have a child on the autism spectrum, others in the family may find small talk hard, struggle with eye contact, and so on. You may find you are supporting the very same vulnerabilities in your child that you have. Keeping this in mind is important, particularly when you are learning a new skill – it can be stressful to be out of your comfort zone.

These conversations could form a life story book for looked-after children

The concepts in this book could be used to deliver best practice for looked-after children and form the beginning of a life story book. In addition to photos of previous carers and memory boxes, a life story book helps children make sense of their past and develop new and secure relationships as they navigate their life challenges. Many of the conversation topics are particularly suitable for life story work, though carers may be sensitive about introducing others (for example, 'Really Rubbish' in Part 2), depending on a young person's recent experiences and readiness to talk through their potentially traumatic past. We recommend that you repeat conversations and review children's previous conversations as this will contribute to the development of a trusting relationship if there has been discontinuity of care in their early years. We use the terms 'family' and 'parents' (the grown-ups in charge) in the broadest sense, but it may be important to modify the language so it is appropriate for a young person's circumstances.

Never ask a question unless…

You know the old saying 'Never ask a question unless you are prepared to hear the answer'? It's true. If you ask your child how things are going, you might get an answer for which you were unprepared. Maybe they will say they hate school. Maybe they will say they are feeling really unhappy. While we all wish for our kid's health and happiness, life isn't like that all the time. There will be times when your child feels miserable, lonely, jealous or spiteful – it's important to accept that negative emotions will be part of your child's life at some point. Having these emotions is not a reflection on your parenting. It's life. It might feel a big ask to 'sit with' your child's difficult emotions; but if you can, it says 'I accept you and all your feelings'. At first, it could feel counter to our instincts because so much of parenting, particularly in the early years, is about helping, protecting or sorting out on behalf of our vulnerable children. Nor are we suggesting you be uncaring or ignore negative emotions; instead, try to accept them in a loving way.

Sometimes we hear parents in therapy sessions trying to shut down their child when they say, for example, that they hate their life. 'Oh, don't say that' is a parent's plaintive cry. This is understandable because there is no doubt it is painful to hear your child is feeling bad. However, think about the message it sends, which is essentially: 'I can't hear about your problems, I don't want to know if you are struggling.' If you can resist trying to erase the 'bad' emotions, you will provide a space for discussion so that your child can figure out why they feel jealous, or catch the thought that makes them dread school – to achieve this is a parenting victory of enormous proportions. If adults around a child convey a sense that this type of open communication is okay, it's very containing (a therapy expression, which means a child will feel calmed knowing there is a grown-up who can deal with and isn't overwhelmed by the situation). We're not pretending this is easy, nor are we suggesting it isn't worrying, but it is part of parenting and a crucial one at that. No one promised you a rose garden.

Tough times? Climb into the pit with your child

Parents often tell us that they are worried about how to respond when their child talks about difficult feelings. Here is a strategy that is both simple and highly effective: First, stop and listen (which is much harder than it sounds). Second, describe what your child has just said (so they know you heard them), and then say something that lets them know you recognize they are having a hard time. Notice that this is very different from making any judgement (positive or negative) about what happened, trying to fix it or describing where they went wrong. Simply empathizing is very powerful and healing, as social scientist Brené Brown notes. Inspired by her narrative, we describe this as 'getting in the pit' together. There may be a time when you problem solve or you act on your child's behalf to change something that is persistently bothering them, but getting in the pit is a good default first step and often *all* that is required. Knowing that your problems are heard and that 'my problem is our problem' is a key part of human connection. If you jump straight to problem solving, you will have missed a crucial opportunity to connect at an emotional level. You can probably identify with this: let's say you have been at home alone with your young children on a rainy day, without any adult company. The children have been acting up, you have been irritable and you are all frazzled. When you tell your partner about your day, the very last thing you want from them is a perky list of fail-safe child management strategies. What you really want is for your partner to stop, really think about how you feel, and *care* about the fact that you had a horrible day.

When to ask for professionals' help

It is to be expected that there will be periods in your child's life when things don't go well, when they feel bad for a few days or a week or two; but if there is *persistent* distress, you might need professional support. It is relatively unusual for significant mental health problems to emerge in middle childhood, but there are instances when consulting a mental health professional is wise – for example, if your child is overwhelmed day after day for several weeks, or there is a significant change in demeanour from their usual approach to life. You can consult your GP in the first instance. If necessary, they will refer you to a specialized mental health team known as the Child and Adolescent Mental Health Service (CAMHS) in the UK, or Children, Youth and Family Mental Health Services in the USA.

Asking about a problem won't create a problem

Whatever the issue is, be reassured that talking about it will not create a problem. Psychiatrist Dan Siegel's superb work points to the idea that a conversation is a sort of 'sorting space' for emotional development, allowing us to organize and manage feelings so that they are neither overwhelming and dominate our thoughts, nor suppressed and find other unhealthy paths of expression such as violence or depression. Parents sometimes worry that simply asking a question about something will somehow put ideas into their child's head, but this is not the case. For example, at the very serious end of the spectrum, let's imagine a child might feel so distressed that they want to harm themselves. Asking about these feelings means you are conveying the idea that you can talk about the difficult stuff, you are ready to hear, and that you care. It starts the conversation and is the first step towards positive change.

Chapter 4

The Wellbeing Compass

Before you get talking, the last item on our agenda in Part 1 is an introduction to the four topics of conversation on the 'wellbeing compass' and their value in relationship building. Then, you and your child will be all set to dive into the *Incredible Conversations*.

The four compass points are:

1. Who are you?
2. How are you?
3. What helps?
4. What gets in the way?

1. Who are you?

These conversations tend to be upbeat, parents create a framework to help children figure out what is true for them, who they are and who they want to be.

Give your child the sense that whoever they are is okay with you

Parents know their children – of course they do – but this section is an invitation to ask about how children see *themselves*, their likes and dislikes, hopes, dreams and fears, all of which are part of 'their story'. Giving children the opportunity to figure out who they are is a hot topic in the current wellbeing literature. These conversations will also enrich your understanding of each other (in our experience, parents almost invariably find out new information about their child). It is a positive dynamic because your child will be left with a sense that you want to *know* them, something that is often felt deeply by parents but remains unsaid.

The ideal scenario is one in which the way children 'present' themselves to the world is pretty much the same as how they feel inside. If there is a major mismatch, it may mean they are vulnerable to self-esteem problems. For example, a child might describe themselves as having a particular attribute, even though they don't quite believe it, because it is highly valued in the family. We also know that self-esteem may be more vulnerable during major life events (like starting school) or at certain stages of development. Most children go through phases of over-identifying with their same-sex parent at around 5 or 6 years old, while in adolescence they may well reject everything their parents stand for. As young people are going through these stages, before they settle into a steady self-concept, we can encourage positive self-esteem by showing them 'unconditional positive regard' (a term coined by Carl Rogers many years ago). It means, essentially, that whoever or whatever you are, it's okay with me. So, a parent might come from a long line of sports fanatics and love fitness themselves, but sport really doesn't feel like fun for their child. Parents can show in words and actions that it's okay to find a different passion. If their kid isn't sporty, it certainly doesn't mean that their parent loves them any less.

No one would argue that parents have a major part to play in shaping their children's identity. Stories we are told about ourselves, play a part in forming our identity. In fact, key therapies such as Narrative Therapy are based on stories. (Narrative Therapy is a talking therapy founded by Michael White that uses the power of personal stories to support change.) Think about those family anecdotes that parents tell their children about their toddler selves, often retold again and again like a ritual. What is the message in that story ? Are some family members painted as heroes and others as troublemakers? This is important because the child described as an 'absolute terror of a toddler' might just take that on board and consider themselves a terror now and forever more. It works both ways because a child described as 'the clever one' may find it really difficult to say that they are struggling with their work. Evidence is emerging that these family stories take on a new importance in the teenage years. While this is undoubtedly powerful, it does not mean that it is set in stone – a good example of a growth mindset (see Chapter 2) having a profound effect in life, not just the classroom. Things change. Family stories can be re-told, and new stories giving a different message can be shared.

Parents' reaction to their child's temperament also plays a part in shaping identity. Temperament covers emotional differences (such as being on the shy side), ways of thinking (such as a tendency towards impulsivity) or actions (such as persistence). These traits are often recognizable in a person across their life span, but can also change according to what they are doing and how others respond to them. Sometimes being outgoing has advantages, but in another situations, it could land you in trouble. For parents, there is a fine line to tread in terms of accepting a child as they come on the one hand, and having a healthy growth mindset to help them develop, capitalize on their strengths and acknowledge their vulnerabilities, on the other. So, it's not asking much then?

With age, children describe themselves in more complex and abstract ways

Very young children will often describe themselves and others in terms of what they can see in front of them. They may also describe their abilities in terms of what they'd *like* to be able to do, rather than what they can *actually* do. By the primary/elementary school years, children start to describe other non-observable aspects of themselves, but these tend to be rather 'all or nothing' statements (for example, 'I hate soup') and they start to compare themselves with their peers, which may be reflected in their self-image. After puberty, self-concept becomes much more abstract and young people understand that roles change and there may be different version of 'a self', depending on the circumstances and people around.

Sshh (sometimes)

Children often need a bit of wiggle room to formulate ideas, particularly for a new idea such as self-concept. It's really tempting to dive in and offer options when no response is forthcoming (parents are programmed to help their children, after all), but the danger is that children are likely to agree with parents' suggestions because they think that's the best thing to do. Try saying things like 'Take your time' or 'This is a tricky question' or 'You can figure it out'. They keep the atmosphere warm, but are not unduly influencing.

> In a nutshell: Who are you?
> It takes time to know yourself. Many adults would say that they are still figuring it out. First, you have to sort out what is true for you, then find ways of expressing that without fear of disappointment or disapproval from significant others, and finally, you 'own it'. It means you can stand up and say, as that *Greatest Showman* song goes, 'This is me'.

2. How are you?

These conversations help children think about the full range of emotions – the good, the bad and the ugly. It introduces the idea of sharing difficult feelings as well as all the good stuff. Make it a safe place to talk and bring it on.

Understanding emotions is a skill we need to learn, just like anything else

Emotions are constructed by our experiences. The same arrangement of facial features can stand for different emotions, depending on where in the world you grow up. The way we label an emotion and understand different aspects of emotions in others, can define our wellbeing, as Lisa Feldman Barrett discusses in her book *How Emotions Are Made* (see 'Further Reading'). The brain is *plastic*, which means that with persistence and patience we can 'relabel' the same sensation as a different emotion. This is where you come in – you can teach your children how to label feelings, and even *re-label* emotions in exactly the same way as you teach them to cross the road. Start with something simple and repeat it *a lot*.

There is strong evidence that being aware of emotions gives you emotional self-control. Labelling your own (or your child's) emotion with a word helps to increase emotional understanding and with it the capacity to manage and express emotions appropriately (so-called 'emotional regulation'). Supporting a child to learn emotional regulation is equivalent to winning the Nobel Prize in Parenting. Naming an emotion helps the brain calm down more quickly when we are in distress, and we can actually *see it happen* as we watch a person's brain react in an MRI (brain) scanner as they feel more settled. This highlights the importance of discussing distressing emotions (such as anger or sadness) as much as positive feelings. The more we can differentiate between shades of emotion, the more flexible we can become in understanding emotions, which all adds up to a high quality of emotional wellbeing. Young children will not have a full range of emotional literacy at first (that would not be expected until well into adolescence); in addition to needing fully mature cognitive skills, people also need *practice*. Every book lover had to learn to read first. They likely had parents who spent time practising phonics with them in the early years and many, many hours discussing the books they adored and the books they didn't. The principle is the same in emotional literacy.

Development of emotions

The seven 'basic' emotions of disgust, happiness, fear, anger, sadness, interest and surprise are around at birth. Even the youngest of infants can pick up emotion in others, but the primary/elementary school years are a time when children become able to describe and understand a wider range of different emotions. They are all simply variations on the basic seven – for example, hatred is a combination of anger and disgust. Using words to convey an abstract concept such as emotion is a pretty philosophical exercise. If you have been 'paying attention in class' (see 'Using visual material is perfect for helping primary/elementary school-age children communicate' in Chapter 2), you will know that this type of task is hard for children before adolescence, so dig in because it will take time. More subtle changes also happen over time. For example, early primary/elementary school-age children begin to grasp that the feelings someone shows may not be the same as their emotions on the inside. The relationship between emotions develops too: younger children may describe having one emotion after another in succession, then they start to understand that they may feel different emotions at the same time. By the teenage years, most young people will be able to describe ambivalence about a specific person or event. Phew. We are exhausted just writing about it...

Anything goes

If children describe a difficult time, get in the pit together (see Chapter 3). Think about how you respond to positive emotions too. Of course, you want to share in the happy times (and so you should) but make sure your child doesn't feel 'rewarded' when they say they feel great or else you are giving them the message that you'd prefer to hear the good stuff. We want children to get the idea that you represent a safe place to think anything through together. You want to telegraph 'I want to hear how you are, however you are'.

Sshh (sometimes)

If your child says things aren't going well, remember to try to sit on the urge to fix it. You could say a few encouraging phrases, such as 'Tell me more... I'm glad you are talking about it,' but otherwise hold fire for a bit. You never know, they might talk *themselves* around or find to an appropriate solution, which is exactly what we are after.

> ### In a nutshell: How are you?
> This topic of conversation helps your child learn to think through how they feel and find ways to describe it in a calm and safe environment.

3. What helps?

These conversations are all about sorting through the resources, tools and support that we use (or could use) when times are tough. They are a chance to talk about challenging times and think about them in a different way.

Stress is a part of life and we have to learn how to manage it

When life throws a challenge at us, whether that is joining a new club, learning a language or something upsetting like losing a loved one, we have to find a way through to cope with the stress.

Embrace the brief times outside your comfort zone
Brace yourself for a bombshell: we recommend *everyone* to feel stress now and then. Stress has got a bad reputation; probably because in the 1930s, eminent scientist Hans Selye proclaimed that stress killed his lab rats more often than any disease. The idea took hold and so 'stress' became synonymous with 'harm'. But, stress is a sign that we need to find an extraordinary response to manage the

challenge in front of us, and so we get a boost of extra energy in the body. It means a new way of dealing with life, often in the form of new skills and knowledge. So, a quick burst of stress is okay, beneficial even. While we suggest positively embracing brief time outside your comfort zone, we do not recommend experiencing chronic stress that is overwhelming and perpetual, day after day. That sort of toxic stress is indeed truly harmful, particularly for young people's developing brains.

Believe stress is helpful and your brain makes the most of the learning opportunity

Here's another idea we think is nothing short of revolutionary: the way we perceive stress changes the way our brain responds to it. If we *just believe* that stress is a sign of performance-enhancing energy, rather than being harmful, our brain reacts differently and is more likely to lay down new circuits and learn from that experience. It means brain growth and emotional growth. For example, if our stomach is churning before a performance, we can describe it as 'stage fright' and fret about the possible impact on our performance. Alternatively, we can label exactly the same physical sensation, in exactly the same situation, as 'extra energy' and notice that this is the body's way of rising to a new occasion before we move briskly onto the stage. Understanding this, and finding the 'sweet-spot' stress level, unlocks new resources and has well established long-term benefits for physical and mental wellbeing.

Not all coping strategies are good coping strategies

When we are faced with a stressful situation (whether the 'good mind stretching' sort or the harmful chronic sort) we need to find a way to respond to the challenge. Say you are lying in bed, at night, feeling afraid of the dark; you might cope with an action (putting on the light) or a thought (I have been in the dark before and it was okay). Of course, not all coping styles are positive; in fact, you might argue that putting the light on is an avoidant strategy, because you never learn that the dark is okay. Children may need support understanding that some responses to stress might feel good in the short term but may not ultimately be the best way forward (for example, eating a whole bag of sweets to boost your energy when you feel tired).

The brilliance of resilience

Learning to cope with stress is vital for long-term wellbeing and here's why: COVID-19 has taught us that almost nothing in life is guaranteed. However, one thing *is* for sure: we will all encounter stress at one time or another in our lifetime. If we are lucky, the first stresses we deal with in our life are minor. Over time we need to figure out our useful coping strategies, pin down the resources that help us and leave aside the things that don't, so that when we face a major stress like bereavement, we have both the skill set and the lived experience to know that we will get through it. Understanding this may be a conscious process, but more likely we are unaware of it at first, and of course this is particularly true of children. Smaller stresses are like inoculations against the big stuff, and we need to experience minor challenges or we would be floored by major life events. You see, stress is not so much the issue; rather, learning to *adapt to it* is. Healthy coping skills are closely linked to better academic performance, social connection, wellbeing and a generally resilient mindset.

Children learn to manage stress with their parents and from their parents
The way babies and their parents relate to each other helps infants learn to manage their first stresses and challenges. Babies use that 'lens' to manage stress in other relationships as they get older. Digby Tantam, a British psychiatrist, describes this continuing relationship as a 'Bluetooth connection' between emotional centres of the child's and parent's brain that persists through life. Isn't that a cracking analogy? Melanie Zimmer-Gembeck sifted through the scientific literature and concluded that our relationship with our parents as toddlers has a small but consistent link with our lifelong coping style. While we don't underestimate the fundamental importance of early parent–child relationships (look at Peter Fonagy's body of work, for example), we also want to underline that family relationships are always evolving and can be strengthened (or damaged) at *any point* in development, however old you are.

With age, children use a wider range of coping strategies

Young children become increasingly proactive and start to select coping strategies as they progress through primary/elementary school. Strategies might include being able to reframe a stressful event (for example, 'My pet was very ill, so he wasn't having a good life – it was kinder to put him to sleep'), use calming talk (for example, 'Everyone forgets lines in a play now and again') or bring a loved one to mind, for support (for example, 'Mum says I can do it, so it'll be okay'), but the range of coping approaches and figuring out their effectiveness continues to develop well into adulthood.

Anything goes

Everyone will have their own idea of what is stressful, and what devastates one person might barely make an impression on another. There are a bewildering number of areas of life that might be considered stressful: it could be feeling ill, having a fight, trying to remember something, missing out on a party invitation, or seeing a loved one in distress. They all count.

Be patient

Often we are not aware of our coping styles, even though we may use them daily. Bringing them to mind, possibly for the first time, takes effort. Expect to hear a lot of '*don't knows*' the first time you talk this through together, but try not to offer suggestions – just sit tight and see what happens.

> **In a nutshell: What helps?**
> Noticing there are ups as well as downs in life is important because it shows that difficult times pass. We also want to sort through the available tools and support that will help us get through tough times.

4. What gets in the way?

To some degree these are the most challenging conversations because they focus on areas that get in the way of our lives. However, they are an important part of family conversation. This is a supported, structured and gentle start to exploring obstacles and ways around them.

Talking about what gets in your way is the first step to making changes

This is a topic that is often avoided in family conversations, despite being a valuable discussion with very powerful positive effects. This is the gist: 'What gets in your way or has tripped you up?' Having this sort of conversation is fundamental to a strong relationship. You could consider these conversations a test case: what does it feel like to discuss hard subjects in your family? If it feels okay for both of you, you open the door to a new level of connection and sharing. Parents of teenagers will be nodding furiously right now because it is the golden ticket into the world of parenting teenagers. It goes something like this: nothing is off the table, bring your worries, your mistakes home, and then we can figure it out in a safe-place, learn from it and avoid it happening again.

Step one is noticing *what* gets in the way. This is really hard so we are not expecting extraordinary results, we are just starting the conversation. If we come up with the obstacles ourselves, it is *much more* likely to invite change than hearing a list generated by someone else, which could be

50

soul-destroying or even potentially damaging. Step two may not always be possible, but sometimes we can move forward using a new approach. We know from our therapeutic experience that simply talking about it – and *that is all* – often means we can get unstuck and try something different. For some people, the roadblocks are worries; others might rush at something with such enthusiasm that things go awry. There might be times when what other people say or do (often with the best of intentions) means we lose track of our goal, make a bad decision or perhaps get fed up and give up. There may be a pattern, things that might get in the way time after time. This is important as if it is 'just a habit' (and almost half of our day-to-day activity is habitual), it is great news because habits can be changed.

Self-reflection is a skill and it takes time to develop

The ability to reflect on ourselves is a developmental process. The part of the brain involved in this is still developing up until the age of about 25, so adjust your expectations accordingly. Children often echo what they have heard adults around them say, but we don't want an echo chamber – we want to encourage the ability to self-reflect and a recognition that some strategies might work better than others.

Sshh (sometimes)

You will be doing something wonderful and supportive by praising any attempt from children to mention things that get in their own way, but try really hard to avoid *adding* to the list of concerns and obstacles.

In a nutshell: What gets in the way?
This is not about pointing out each others' mistakes, this is an invitation to reflect on ourselves, ask what gets in our way and maybe what we would like to do differently. It's the beginning of a long term, possibly lifelong project.

---

* * *

Mindset in gear? You are ready to go live...

There is a lot to take in, but remember this is a journey and journeys take time. So, read, reflect and come back to this mindset section as often as you can. Perhaps focus on just one or two conversation tips if a lot of the ideas are new to you. Don't beat yourself up if you find a conversation hasn't gone smoothly; instead, congratulate yourself for having another go. If you notice you took an approach that we might not have recommended, consider it a plus that you spotted it. A good catch, as they say.

Now, go and find your small conversation partner, and Get Your Incredible On...

PART 2

The Incredible Conversations

Share your experience, have a conversation
and build your relationship, together

Compass Point 1: Who Are You?

These conversations tend to be upbeat. Parents create a framework to help children figure out what is true for them, who they are and who they want to be.

It takes time to know yourself. Many adults would say that they are still figuring it out. First you have to figure out what is true for you, then you have to find ways of expressing that without fear of disappointment or disapproval from significant others, and finally you 'own it'. It means you can stand up and say – as that song from *The Greatest Showman* goes – 'This is me'.

Who are you? My Best Day

An easy start, usually fun and full of positivity – a way of finding out about people, places and things that are loved or wished for.

This is as much about children pausing to ask themselves what they really love as it is about parents getting to know what children love. It is an invitation to get to know ourselves, as self-knowledge is the bedrock of wellbeing.

Playing Minecraft® and eating jammy doughnuts all day in a onesie might not be your idea of a good time, but we want answers that are true and authentic, so no editing of children's answers from parents, please. Anything goes. This conversation is not about a life goal, or an indication of how life will turn out. **It's just about having fun.**

Who are you? My Best Day

An easy start, usually fun and full of positivity – a way of finding out about people, places and things that are loved or wished for.

Conversation starters

- Let's imagine you can do ANYTHING you like for a day.

- Talk me through your day, minute by minute.

- Do you wake up in a treehouse, play with kittens, fly a helicopter and have a foam-slide party?

- You can choose anything, invite anyone to be with you, be anywhere, do anything for one day. Ready? Go...

Keep talking

We don't want anything edited out, but we always want to hear more details, so try this:

- What happens the second you open your eyes and wake up?

- Are you in your usual bed?

- What happens next?

- You open the door of the bedroom, and then...

- Where are you now?

- Who else is there?

- What do you eat?

- Do you have superpowers?

- Where do you sleep?

- I have extra 'magic' hours in the day... Is there anything else to do?

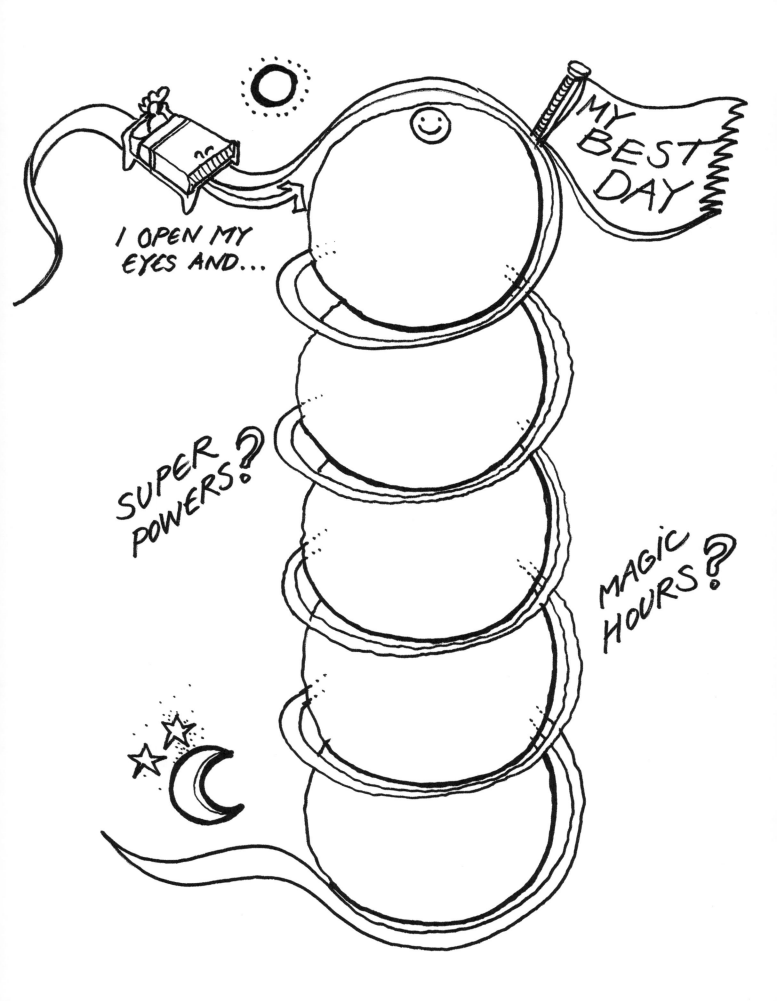

Who are you? My Best Day

An easy start, usually fun and full of positivity – a way of finding out about people, places and things that are loved or wished for.

Whoohoo! One **Incredible Conversation** in the bag.

The majority of children will have had enough after a conversation and might want to go off elsewhere and release some energy. **So, mark the conversation with a fist bump boom** here and now (or whatever little ritual you choose to use) and bag it as a success.

For kids who still have time or energy to spare, circle one of the faces to show what you thought of this conversation, or do your own drawing.

Parents, use this as a place to reflect on the conversation you had together:

Date of conversation . . . .

Home/school/significant events that are happening now

. . . .

How do you think it went?

. . . .

. . . .

What would you take from it?

. . . .

. . . .

Anything else you want to remember?

. . . .

. . . .

Who are you? Think of a Link

A conversation about similarities (and differences) between family and others in our world – ideas about who we are or what we could become often pop up.

Part of understanding who we are involves making comparisons between ourselves and others – it's an important part of growing up and figuring out who we are. It can be fun to notice similarities between ourselves and family members or friends. Whether something makes us seem the same as or different to others, it's important to welcome similarities and differences equally. You might hear, 'Oh, you are so like Aunt Laura – you both hate maths,' but maybe that means maths is dismissed as a strength, prematurely. It's good to be able to coax out these ideas, particularly where links have been made that could shut down opportunities or give us negative views about ourselves. We can only rewrite unhelpful stories or challenge muddled-up ideas when they are brought to mind and said aloud, so let's get to it.

Younger children most often make comparisons based on what they look like. As they get older and into the teenage years, comparisons become more abstract and identifications more complicated. In the teenage years, young people may distance themselves from others because of their personal attributes or approaches to life. Both these are normal and part of growing up.

Who are you? Think of a Link

A conversation about similarities (and differences) between family and others in our world – ideas about who we are or what we could become often pop up.

Conversation starters

- We are all alike in some ways and different in others.

- Some parts of us (the way we look or act) might be similar to family or friends.

- Write your name or draw yourself in the middle of the picture.

- Draw some people in your life that are like you in one way or another – think about home, school or anywhere else.

- Make a link, between you and them and tell me (or draw) what makes you the same. There is an example in the illustration opposite to help you get started.

Keep talking

- Are you the same because of how you look?

- What about the things you like doing?

- You could be alike because of how you act.

- Are you linked by the way other people describe you both?

- What about things that make you different?

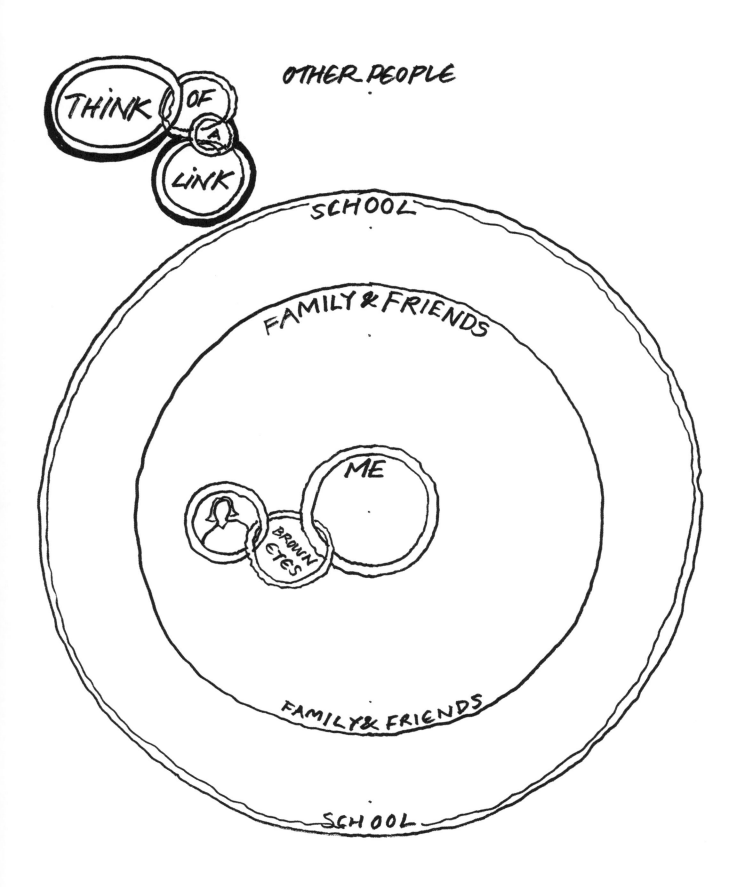

OTHER PEOPLE

THINK OF A LINK

SCHOOL

FAMILY & FRIENDS

ME

BROWN EYES

FAMILY & FRIENDS

SCHOOL

OTHER PEOPLE

Who are you? Think of a Link

A conversation about similarities (and differences) between family and others in our world – ideas about who we are or what we could become often pop up.

If you get the message 'I don't want to talk right now,' but it's delivered in an appropriate way, **give that a fist bump**. (Hello? 'Excellent emotional regulation' alert.)

Of course, if you did get a conversation going, fist bump that too. Children are likely to need a break after each conversation. If they would like to, they can write or draw what they thought of this conversation here.

Parents, use this as a place to reflect on the conversation you had together:

Date of conversation . . . .

Home/school/significant events that are happening now

. . . .

How do you think it went?

. . . .

. . . .

What would you take from it?

. . . .

. . . .

Anything else you want to remember?

. . . .

. . . .

Who are you? Memory Frame Game

A focus on the good old times. Talking about a favourite memory is a great bonding experience and can be a superb distraction for worriers.

Asking someone about their favourite memory means you get to know one another on another level. Parents are often surprised by this conversation because it could be an event that was apparently incidental that is close to their child's heart. Sharing for sharing's sake is the cement that bonds relationships. Interestingly, mothers and children are more likely than other family members to share memories, but we would recommend a walk down memory lane for all the family now and again.

This conversation has a **secret added bonus**. Drifting back into a good memory is an absorbing distraction activity, particularly for kids who tend to worry. To make it really effective, use all five senses in minute detail. By taking a deep dive into the episode, our brain has to work harder to pull all the parts of the memory together, leaving less headspace to worry. For example, a day at the beach might involve remembering the feeling of the wet sand on your feet, the smell of the suntan lotion, the shape of the sun through the orange sun shade, the taste of the salt from the waves, the sound of the wind rattling the windbreak and so on. You can pull this memory exercise out, like a rabbit from a hat, at any time. It's a go-to good place that can be used for relaxation or distraction whenever you want. If a memory gets a bit repetitive, think of a different one or imagine a fantasy scenario (see 'Who are you? My Best Day' for inspiration).

Who are you? Memory Frame Game

A focus on the good old times. Talking about a favourite memory is a great bonding experience and can be a superb distraction for worriers.

Conversation starters

- One of my favourite memories is [insert memory]. What's yours? It might be a special day like a birthday, or just a day that you loved...just because.

- The trick here is to remember all the tiny details about it.

- The picture frame has little reminders for all five senses. Shut your eyes, then imagine stepping back into the memory and look around you.

- What can you **see**? Look up, look down and behind you.

- What can you **smell**? Take a deep breath in through your nose and out through your mouth and remember.

- What can you **feel**? What is around you? In your mind, reach out and touch something else in your memory.

- What can you **hear**? Think about quiet sounds as well as loud ones.

- What about **taste**? Maybe you had something special to eat?

- Now, draw a picture or write down a word for each of these senses.

Keep talking

- I wonder why it was a special time for you?

- Can you remember anything else about this? What would that be?

Who are you? Memory Frame Game

A focus on the good old times. Talking about a favourite memory is a great bonding experience and can be a superb distraction for worriers.

 Whether it lasts a few seconds or goes on **for ages**, any conversation counts. Quick ones are a bit like warming up your communication muscles.

Long or short, after each conversation, children are likely to need a break, but there may be kids who would like to write or draw their thoughts about the conversation. Do it here.

Parents, use this as a place to reflect on the conversation you had together:

Date of conversation . . . .

Home/school/significant events that are happening now

. . . .

How do you think it went?

. . . .

. . . .

What would you take from it?

. . . .

. . . .

Anything else you want to remember?

. . . .

. . . .

Who are you? Wishful Thinking

An old favourite, this conversation gets at what might make life better if only we had a magic wand. It's a good one for children who find it hard to say what is bothering them.

Some children wish for no homework or for fewer arguments at home; others would like a chocolate fountain or for an end to global conflict. Any answer is valid and shows a hint of what might be on a child's mind, day to day.

You know the old saying, never ask a question unless you want to know the answer? If children's wishes are of the 'chocolate fountain' variety, it might well be an indication that things are okay right now. If there is something more serious on the list, take it as a real compliment because it shows there is enough trust between you and your child for them to share something that might be a concern.

Who are you? Wishful Thinking

An old favourite, this conversation gets at what might make life better if only we had a magic wand. It's a good one for children who find it hard to say what is bothering them.

Conversation starters

- You've got three wishes. You can wish for anything you like.
  - Draw or write them.
  - Now tell me all about them.

Keep talking

- I wonder why you went for wish number 1.
- Tell me more about wish number 2 – why would life be better?
- What about wish number 3?
- If I had a magic wand, what else would you change?
- If we could magic something to appear, what would it be?
- If we could use magic to make something disappear, what would you pick?
- Can you guess **my** three wishes?

Who are you? Wishful Thinking

An old favourite, this conversation gets at what might make life better if only we had a magic wand. It's a good one for children who find it hard to say what is bothering them.

However the conversation goes, **end it with your ritual**. Some of the most Incredible Moments happen in the spaces in between conversations.

Is your kid still raring to go, pen in hand? They can write or draw comments about this conversation here.

Parents, use this as a place to reflect on the conversation you had together:

Date of conversation . . . .

Home/school/significant events that are happening now

. . . .

How do you think it went?

. . . .

. . . .

What would you take from it?

. . . .

. . . .

Anything else you want to remember?

. . . .

. . . .

Who are you? Next Up...

Future visions say a lot about how we feel about ourselves right now. This is an invitation to talk together about who, what and where the future might be.

Talking about the future with children sometimes gets a bit focused on jobs. This can get a bit tired for a number of reasons, not least because Generation Z (and their successors, Generation Alpha) will live in a world with much more career flexibility than in the olden days. There are so many other facets of life that are valuable, and if grown-ups don't give these 'air-time', children might get the message that other parts of their life don't count (see Chapter 4, 'Who are you?' if you are in any doubt about that). Quite apart from this, it is positively enthralling to hear a child's thoughts and ideas for any and all aspects of their life plan.

Whatever their future plan is, go with it. Parents are often such realists (very possibly for good reason) that it inhibits future vision. No one needs to worry just yet about how the mortgage will be paid.

Who are you? Next Up...

Future visions say a lot about how we feel about ourselves right now. This is an invitation to talk together about who, what and where the future might be.

Conversation starters

- Imagine you are a grown-up. Pick a grown-up age and let's draw it out and talk as you go. You could make a mind map if you prefer.

Shhh. Parents, don't say anything else just yet...

Keep talking

If it's hard to get going, use these ideas:

- Where are you living?

- Do you have a flat or a house? Maybe you live in a houseboat?

- Who do you live with?

- Do you have a partner? What's your partner like?

- Do you have children? Tell me about them.

- What will you do at weekends?

- Will you have pets?

- Where will you go on holiday?

You can have a bit of fun with this and ask about what life might look like at different ages, or bring it closer to the present. What might happen next year, or in secondary school?

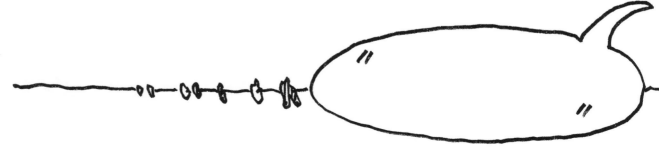

Who are you? Next Up...

Future visions say a lot about how we feel about ourselves right now. This is an invitation to talk together about who, what and where the future might be.

Another conversation, another bond made. Celebrate, and then invite kids to take a break.

For kids who are up for it, write or draw any thoughts on this conversation here.

Parents, use this as a place to reflect on the conversation you had together:

Date of conversation . . . .

Home/school/significant events that are happening now

. . . .

How do you think it went?

. . . .

. . . .

What would you take from it?

. . . .

. . . .

Anything else you want to remember?

. . . .

. . . .

Who are you? Blowing Bubbles

A conversation about how children think they spend their time in the family. This is all about seeing things from another person's perspective.

An important part of building a relationship and keeping it strong is understanding things from the point of view of the other person in the relationship. Sometimes it's hard to 'get at' what children are thinking unless the setting is right. This conversation is all about how children see their time spent at home. It is not so much about what the actual proportions of time spent on each activity actually are but more about what children **think** they are. It is their experience and that is the value of this conversation.

Older children are more likely to be able to plan this picture so all their activities are covered, but younger children may run out of space because planning takes time to learn (it's a so-called 'executive function' skill). You can still have a meaningful conversation about the different size of their bubbles. Add an extension page if it feels important to add things.

Who are you? Blowing Bubbles

A conversation about how children think they spend their time in the family. This is all about seeing things from another person's perspective.

Conversation starters

- Draw a bubble for each activity in your day at home and with the family.

- The bigger the bubble, the more time you spend doing that thing.

- Try it now...

Shhh. Parents, if you can, just watch and learn...

Keep talking

- You can add as many things as you like but here are some ideas:
    - Fun family times.
    - Arguing.
    - Mealtimes.
    - Chores.
    - Playing.
    - Exercise.
    - Time alone.

- So, most of your time at home is spent doing [find the biggest bubble].

- Could you pop one of these bubbles (and make life different)?

- Are there any more bubbles that you would like to add?

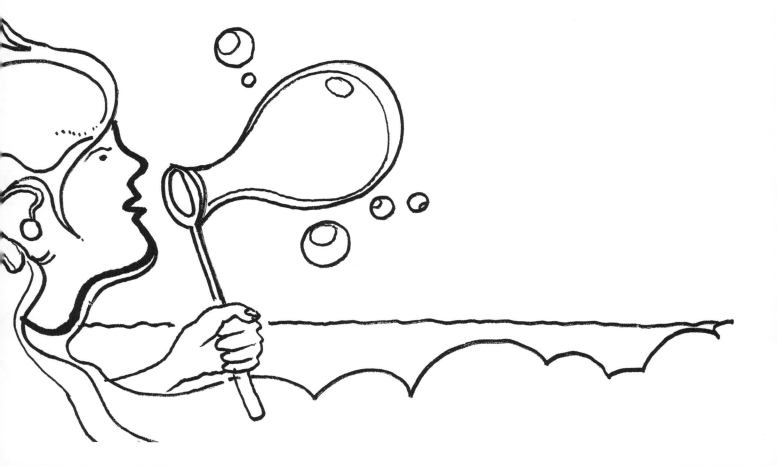

Who are you? Blowing Bubbles

A conversation about how children think they spend their time in the family. This is all about seeing things from another person's perspective.

If you need to round off a conversation before it feels 'finished', mark the pause as a job done. You've started and that's often the hardest part.

Have a breather now. This conversation can sometimes raise big emotions.

Kids can write or draw what they thought of this conversation here if they like (and maybe give it a mark out of 10).

Parents, use this as a place to reflect on the conversation you had together:

Date of conversation . . . .

Home/school/significant events that are happening now

. . . .

How do you think it went?

. . . .

. . . .

What would you take from it?

. . . .

. . . .

Anything else you want to remember?

. . . .

. . . .

Who are you? Piece of Cake

This is a conversation about the different parts of our life, and figuring out which ones matter most to us.

Part of figuring out who you are includes sorting out what matters to you. Susan Harter, an expert on the way children describe themselves, found that if you ask them, children usually describe five different parts of their life: schoolwork, friends and family, physical skills (for example, sport), the way they look and (what grown-ups call) behaviour.

The importance of different slices of life often changes quite a lot as children grow up. For example, younger children might think about their physical abilities a bit more, while older children are often focused on their appearance as they move into adolescence. This is also influenced by what's happening in their life or how adults around them prioritize life. (Remember the fiercely competitive Buddhist monks in Chapter 2?)

Who are you? Piece of Cake

This is a conversation about the different parts of our life, and figuring out which ones matter most to us.

Conversation starters

- Life is made up of different parts – sort of like slices of cake.
- Kids usually say there are five different slices in their life:
  - Friends and family.
  - Schoolwork and school life.
  - The way they look.
  - Being able to do things like catch a ball or do somersaults.
  - What grown-ups call 'behaviour' (running into trouble because of what they say or do).
- Some parts of life might matter to us more than others, or we might feel that all the bits count just as much as the others. Everyone has their own ideas.
- Use the cake to show how much each slice matters to you. A big slice means it matters a lot, a little slice means you don't really mind about it. You could choose a different colour for each slice.

Keep talking

- Which slice makes you feel most proud right now? (Or most often?)
- Are there other slices that you would add?

It's a good sign if you can pin down one area that inspires pride, but if none are forthcoming, don't force it. Perhaps come back to it after a big positive event and talk about it together then.

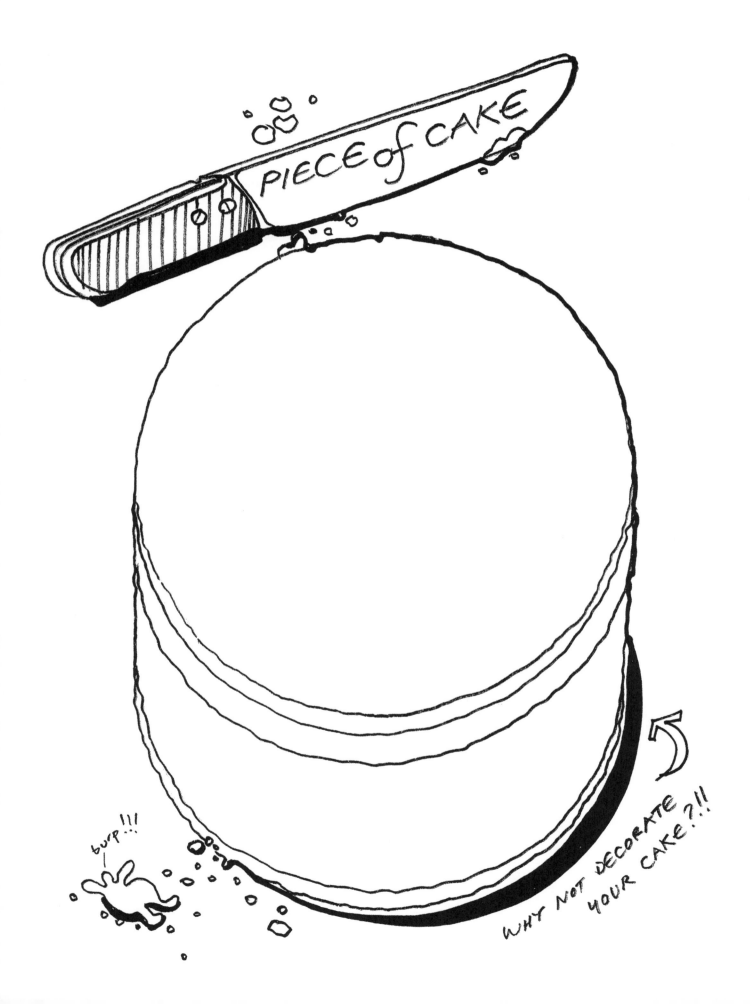

Who are you? Piece of Cake

This is a conversation about the different parts of our life, and figuring out which ones matter most to us.

Celebrate that you had a go together, because **that** is success indeed.

If kids want to, record any thoughts about doing the conversation here. Maybe a thumbs up or thumbs down?

Parents, use this as a place to reflect on the conversation you had together:

Date of conversation . . . .

Home/school/significant events that are happening now

. . . .

How do you think it went?

. . . .

. . . .

What would you take from it?

. . . .

. . . .

Anything else you want to remember?

. . . .

. . . .

Who are you? This Is Me

This pulls together the discussions in 'Who Are You?' and is a chance to think together about how we see ourselves, how we feel inside and how others see us. These parts may be the same or very different.

The way we appear to the world might be different to how we feel inside, and the way we think of ourselves may be different to how others see us. On the other hand, all these different parts might be pretty similar. For example, a young primary/elementary school-age boy may like dressing up, but kids at school say only girls dress up. That young boy may truly decide he doesn't like dressing up after all and stop, or he may hide it from others but still feel like dressing up. Or he may say, 'Tough luck, it works for me,' and don a tiara. It's hard to think about all these bits of ourselves and how others see us, but this is a good place to start.

Who are you? This Is Me

This pulls together the discussions in 'Who Are You?' and is a chance to think together about how we see ourselves, how we feel inside and how others see us. These parts may be the same or very different.

Conversation starters

- Describing yourself is sometimes difficult, so let's think about three ideas to help get us going. Use the picture to draw:
  - How you look (1).
  - How you feel inside (2).
  - How other people see you (3).
- Find number 1 on the page and draw the way you look.
- For number 2, finish these sentences and put your ideas inside the thought bubbles:
  - I like...
  - I hate...
  - I care about...
  - I'm worried about...
  - I get excited about...
  - My traditions are...
- For number 3, look at the audience and write or draw:
  - How your class would describe you.
  - How your teacher would describe you.
  - How [insert a friend's name] would describe you.
  - How [insert family member] would describe you.
  - Add anyone else you want to.

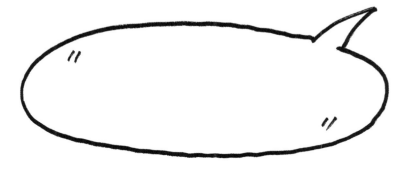

Who are you? This Is Me

This pulls together the discussions in 'Who Are You?' and is a chance to think together about how we see ourselves, how we feel inside and how others see us. These parts may be the same or very different.

 You've started a remarkable conversation, which you can both come back to and discuss for years to come.

This is a big discussion – and a really good example of a work in progress. You may get very little from this conversation at first, but over months and years give it another go and see what the changes might be.

If there's more to say, kids can write or draw what they thought of this conversation here.

Parents, use this as a place to reflect on the conversation you had together:

Date of conversation . . . .

Home/school/significant events that are happening now

. . . .

How do you think it went?

. . . .

. . . .

What would you take from it?

. . . .

. . . .

Anything else you want to remember?

. . . .

. . . .

Compass Point 2: How Are You?

These conversations help you think about the full range of emotions – the good, the bad and the ugly. They introduce us to the idea of sharing difficult feelings as well as all the good stuff. Make this a safe, comfortable place to talk and bring it on.

This topic of conversation helps your child learn to think through how they feel and find ways to describe it in a calm environment.

How are you? Mood Mountain

Sometimes it's hard to describe how you feel. This is an easy way to describe where you are at today, without saying a word.

Let's start simple. Here we use a high mountain or a deep pit (see Chapter 3) to stand for how we feel. It is easy to grasp for any school-age child or for people who are new to the emotion discussion game.

You might be tempted to 'congratulate' someone because they say they are on the summit. It's good to know a loved one is feeling good, but it's important to resist the urge to say 'Well done' as you would be implying that positive feelings are somehow better. This is different from sharing joy together (which we thoroughly recommend).

GROWN-UPS HAVE BAD DAYS TOO

How are you? Mood Mountain

Sometimes it's hard to describe how you feel. This is an easy way to describe where you are at today, without saying a word.

Conversation starters

- Look at the picture. This is mood mountain. The top of the mountain is for when you feel the best ever. Down at the bottom of the page in the pit is for the worst you have ever felt. The person on the ground is for when you feel okay, sort of middling.

- Choose any colour you like. Make a mark to show how you feel today. It might be anywhere from the top of the mountain to the bottom of the pit.

Keep talking

- What would have to happen for you to move from here (farther down the mountain) to here (farther up)?

- How do you **usually** feel, most days?

- When was the last time you were on the summit/in the pit? (This is a chance to notice together that feelings **change**.)

- Let me tell you about a time I was in the pit/on the summit.

How are you? Mood Mountain

Sometimes it's hard to describe how you feel. This is an easy way to describe where you are at today, without saying a word.

If you 'only' choose a colour together to use, it's a success, time together and a conversation started, so mark it and **give it a fist bump**.

If they want to, kids can write or draw what they thought of this conversation here.

Parents, use this as a place to reflect on the conversation you had together:

Date of conversation . . . .

Home/school/significant events that are happening now

. . . .

How do you think it went?

. . . .

. . . .

What would you take from it?

. . . .

. . . .

Anything else you want to remember?

. . . .

. . . .

How are you? How Do You Wheel?

Naming feelings is an important part of sorting them out. It is a powerful tool, and this is a gentle conversation to start the feeling wheel turning.

Being able to find a word for different emotions is very important (see 'How are you?' in Chapter 4). There is a good reason why we use a wheel here. Positive feelings are no more 'valuable' than negative ones, and using a circle shows us that any sort of feeling has an equal place. Remember having a feeling is not the same as acting it out. Notice we suggest using the expression 'the way that people feel'. Talking about the feelings that everyone can have, rather than just our own emotions, frees us up to discuss all the difficult emotions, which evidence tells us is so important for wellbeing.

Very young children may use only 'happy' or 'sad' at first, so thinking of even one other emotion would be superb. (Interestingly, emerging data shows that some adults are also only able to name a handful of emotions.) Parents could make good use of the speech bubble here to note any special words that children use for particular feelings. Use these terms if you spot that feeling in the moment, because naming it, even if it is not a traditional word, still counts.

Anything goes, of course, but take note if the circle is largely populated with either negative or positive feelings, and highlight the opposite sort of feeling from now and then, in family life.

How are you? How Do You Wheel?

Naming feelings is an important part of sorting them out. It is a powerful tool, and this is a gentle conversation to start the feeling wheel turning.

Conversation starters

- This is a wheel. Each bit of the wheel stands for a different feeling.
- You probably won't be able to fill in all the segments, but try and think of as many different words as you can for the way that people feel.
- Add colours or even emoji stickers if you like.

Keep talking

- Do you feel [choose a feeling] sometimes?
- Are there any feelings on the wheel that could get in our way ?
- Which feelings might help us?

Make a colour diary (use a colour for each feeling), then spot which colour happens most often. Show each other your diaries if you can. (PS Watch the film **Inside Out** together – it's an excellent film and we stole this idea from it.)

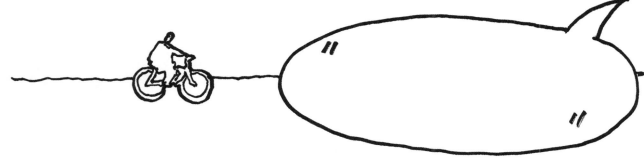

How are you? How Do You Wheel?

Naming feelings is an important part of sorting them out. It is a powerful tool, and this is a gentle conversation to start the feeling wheel turning.

End this conversation feeling good, and you'll want to do it again.

This is one to revisit over and over. Watch the wheel populate with different emotions.

Kids can write or draw what they thought of this conversation here, if they feel like it. Otherwise, call that a job well done.

Parents, use this as a place to reflect on the conversation you had together:

Date of conversation . . . .

Home/school/significant events that are happening now

. . . .

How do you think it went?

. . . .

. . . .

What would you take from it?

. . . .

. . . .

Anything else you want to remember?

. . . .

. . . .

How are you? Playing Detective

We all pick up emotions from each other using 'clues'. This conversation invites a discussion about how different family members express different emotions. It is very useful for kids who struggle with social communication.

We are highly perceptive to other people's feelings. Babies even a few days old pick up their parents' emotional temperature. We send out signals about how we feel in lots of ways: facial expression, body language, tone of voice, words and actions. Children's observation skills are mind-blowing. Some kids can describe their parent's meltdown signs with forensic – and possibly rather wounding – accuracy. Remember we all have bad days whether we are a kid or a grown-up – that's the **whole point** of this book. On the other hand, some people struggle to understand the signs of emotion in others. It's very valuable to get a handle on either position. This conversation unpacks how other people express themselves.

Parents, during this conversation kids might choose to describe you. If the description doesn't make you feel proud, be brave and remember we all have difficult moments from time to time. Try to listen rather than react because this is a chance to learn how your child understands your actions or expressions. Asking how we understand emotions in each other is a thought-provoking and valuable experience.

How are you? Playing Detective

We all pick up emotions from each other using 'clues'. This conversation invites a discussion about how different family members express different emotions. It is very useful for kids who struggle with social communication.

 ## Conversation starters

- When an octopus is stressed, it releases ink. A stressed porcupine raises its quills. People show how they feel in different ways, just like these animals. Some people go a bit quiet when they are worried, others pace up and down. Both these reactions are okay.

- Pick a feeling (Is it in 'How are you? How Do You Wheel?' If not, remember to add it.)

- Choose two people in your life. It could be someone who lives in your home, a teacher, or anyone else.

- Now look at the picture and play detective for **each** of these two people in turn.
    - What sort of thing might that person say when they feel [insert feeling]?
    - What noises do they make?
    - What does their face look like?
    - What sort of thing would they do?

- Now think about what **you** would say or do when you feel that emotion.

 ## Keep talking

- You might even be able to guess what they might be thinking (this is more difficult, so is more suitable for older children to try).

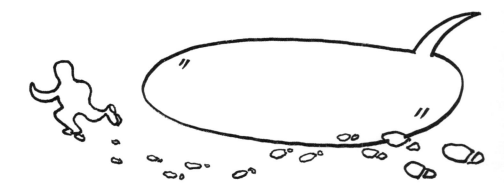

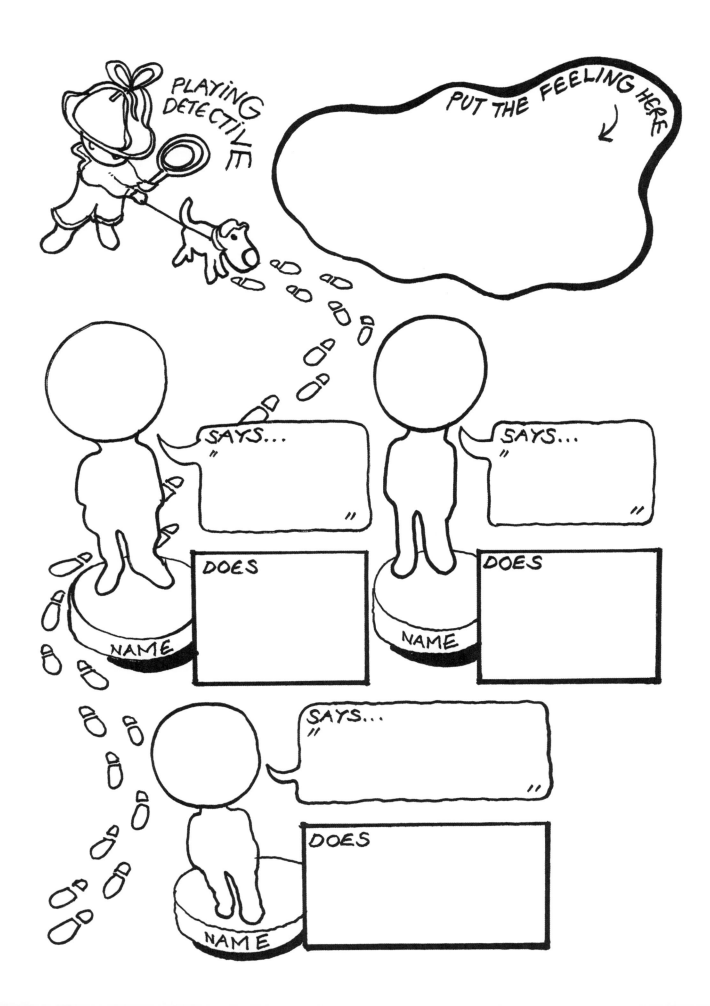

How are you? Playing Detective

We all pick up emotions from each other using 'clues'. This conversation invites a discussion about how different family members express different emotions. It is very useful for kids who struggle with social communication.

 You may be falling about laughing together at the descriptions of a teacher's signs of boredom, or perhaps you are surprised about the aspects of emotional expression that are still a work in progress. Either way, you've nailed it.

This conversation can sometimes be challenging if the focus is on the family, so good for you if you made it, and stayed with it, and were able to listen.

Kids can write or draw any comments about the conversation here (but no pressure, as they will probably have had enough by now).

Parents, use this as a place to reflect on the conversation you had together:

Date of conversation . . . .

Home/school/significant events that are happening now

. . . .

How do you think it went?

. . . .

. . . .

What would you take from it?

. . . .

. . . .

Anything else you want to remember?

. . . .

. . . .

How are you? Worry Pots

This is a chance for children to describe who tends to hold onto a worry in a family, using just pictures. It is brilliant stuff for children who find it hard to find the words.

If there is a worry in the family, who takes it on the most? This conversation never fails to amaze us, because even very young children can often describe family dynamics with extraordinary insight, as long as they have the right props. Taking on a worry is neither a good or a bad thing, but knowing everyone's position helps us understand each other and move forward. For example, a young person may have a perpetually messy room, but if it's not a worry for them, their motivation to change it will be very low. Notice we are not suggesting that it can't be changed, just that our approach would need to be adjusted accordingly. Depending on the issue, different family members will have different views, so try it with a variety of topics. Each member of the family has a 'worry pot'. The more worries in the pot, the more the worries are on that person's mind.

We have seen this conversation idea being used imaginatively on many occasions. For instance, a child might draw an overflowing pot, the contents spilling all over the floor, to indicate that a family member is feeling overwhelmed. They say 'a picture paints a thousand words' and how right they are.

RELATIONSHIP SKILLS MEAN A BETTER FUTURE

How are you? Worry Pots

This is a chance for children to describe who tends to hold onto a worry in a family, using just pictures. It is brilliant stuff for children who find it hard to find the words.

Conversation starters

- Choose 'a thing' that happens in your family. It could be anything, like talking about school tests, planning lunch or monitoring screen time.
- Look at these empty pots. Everyone in the family has their own pot. The fuller the pot, the more worried that person is about 'the thing'.
- Use the pots to show how worried each person is.
- You can draw some more pots if you want to add other people.

Keep talking

- Are there different parts of that thing that worry some people but not others? (For example, one person worries about screen time affecting eyesight, and another person worries that the information is too grown-up.)

WORRY POTS

a lot

half

a bit

NAME

NAME

NAME

NAME

NAME

NAME

How are you? Worry Pots

This is a chance for children to describe who tends to hold onto a worry in a family, using just pictures. It is brilliant stuff for children who find it hard to find the words.

End on a high note.

Give your child the chance to go off and do something else, but if they want to hang around, they can write or draw what they thought of this conversation here.

Parents, use this as a place to reflect on the conversation you had together:

Date of conversation . . . .

Home/school/significant events that are happening now

. . . .

How do you think it went?

. . . .

. . . .

What would you take from it?

. . . .

. . . .

Anything else you want to remember?

. . . .

. . . .

How are you? Heads and Hearts – Step 1

This is all about figuring out the difference between thoughts and feelings. It is great practice for worriers.

Understanding that emotions come from thoughts is an important part of emotional regulation. Simply understanding that thoughts influence feelings is very powerful because it comes with a recognition that 'since I control what I think, I can influence how I feel'. For example: 'I **think** rats are dangerous, so I **feel** frightened when I see one.' Thoughts come first and **lead** to feelings, so we have drawn a thought bubble shaped like number 1 and a feeling heart shaped like number 2.

This is a pretty advanced exercise but such a useful one to introduce because it's a potentially revolutionary skill for wellbeing. Many adults find it hard to differentiate between thoughts and feelings, and harder still to remember that thoughts come before feelings, so adjust your expectations accordingly. Although younger children may not manage this at first, we also know that it is a skill, so practice is the key. If you talk about the differences between a thought and a feeling every time you set the table for dinner, you will have an extremely emotionally articulate child before long.

How are you? Heads and Hearts – Step 1

This is all about figuring out the difference between thoughts and feelings. It is great practice for worriers.

Conversation starters

- What we **think** and how we **feel** are two different things, but sometimes it's difficult to figure them out. Grown-ups get them mixed up too.

- Here are some examples of what I mean: When I went to the dentist last week, I **thought** 'The drill will hurt' and so I **felt** nervous. When I stroked the rabbit yesterday, I **thought** 'The rabbit is so cute' and so I **felt** happy.

- Pick something you did at home or school yesterday and draw or write it at the top of the picture.

- Now see if you can say what you **thought** and how you **felt**, and write or draw that too.

Keep talking

Sometimes the feelings are the most obvious, so you could talk about the feeling and 'chase it back' to catch the thought.

- Let's try this another way around. Name your feeling first of all and **now** try to work backwards to figure out the thought that caused your feeling.

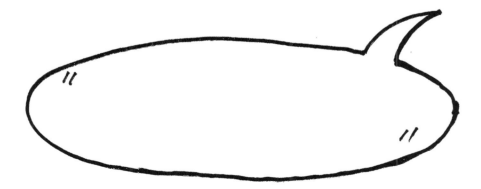

How are you? Heads and Hearts – Step 1

This is all about figuring out the difference between thoughts and feelings. It is great practice for worriers.

Remember the power of a growth mindset – it takes time to learn anything. This might be one to re-visit after a bit if the ideas didn't gel this time.

Kids' comments or ideas about this conversation can be written or drawn here (remember it's just an optional extra). It's also okay to just circle a word to show the thought.

Really good   Okay   Rubbish

Parents, use this as a place to reflect on the conversation you had together:

Date of conversation . . . .

Home/school/significant events that are happening now

. . . .

How do you think it went?

. . . .

. . . .

What would you take from it?

. . . .

. . . .

Anything else you want to remember?

. . . .

. . . .

How are you? Heads and Hearts — Step 2

This conversation introduces the idea that we can decide how we feel, because we can change what we think.

You have the power to decide how you feel. You really can. In 'How are you? Heads and Hearts: Step 1' we used the example of how, on the way to the dentist, you **think,** 'The drill will hurt,' and so you **feel** nervous. However, you can decide what you think and that gives you the power to change how you feel. On the way to the dentist, you could **think,** 'The dentist will check my teeth and make them healthy,' and then you will **feel** calmer and possibly more upbeat.

This one is tricky, so it is likely to work best with older children. If this conversation feels too much at first for younger kids, you can get tuned into the same idea by inserting it into a wellbeing diet of family conversations. So, for example, the next time the car gets a parking ticket, you could think, 'Typical – money down the drain,' and then feel (and act) outraged. An alternative thought might be 'Well, I parked on a double yellow, so I guess it's a fair cop...', resulting in feeling (and acting) acceptance. Talk together about the different ways we can think about the same situation in the moment and how it changes feelings. Modelling is a powerful learning tool (Psst. Parents, go back to Chapter 2 and re-read the section 'Children learn by watching').

How are you? Heads and Hearts – Step 2

This conversation introduces the idea that we can decide how we feel, because we can change what we think.

Conversation starters

- In 'How are you? Heads and Hearts Step 1' we noticed that what we **think** and how we **feel** are two different things.

- Let's go back to the example you chose in Step 1 and change the thought in the thought bubble to something completely different.

- Everything else is the same, but what has happened to the thought?

Keep talking

- Discuss different thoughts for the same event and play around a bit with it. Imagine first thinking, 'It's going to be awful,' and notice how you would feel.

- Now compare that with thinking, 'I've done this lots of times and nothing bad has happened,' and discuss how you might feel after **that** thought.

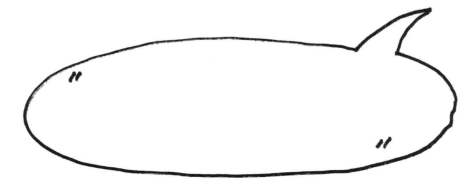

HEADS AND HEARTS

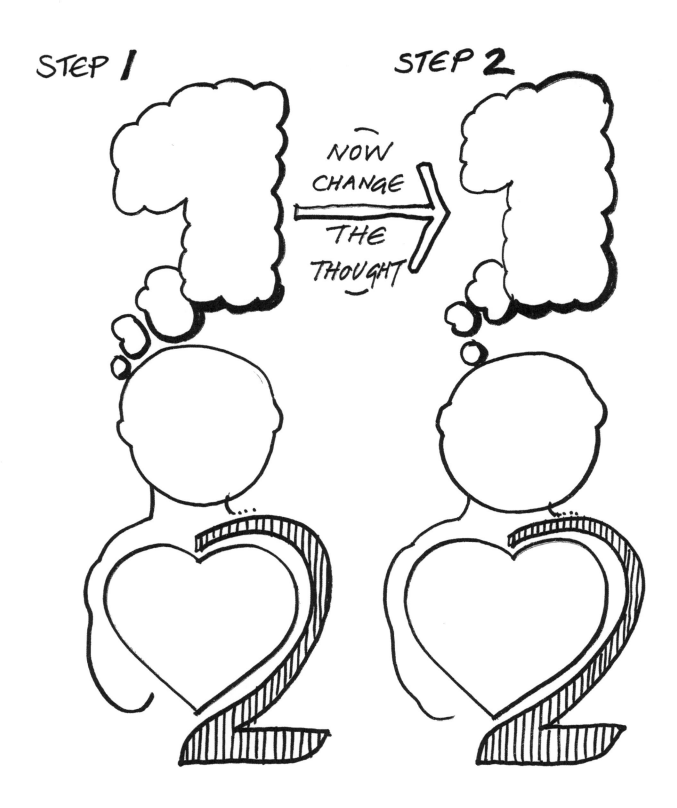

How are you? Heads and Hearts – Step 2

This conversation introduces the idea that we can decide how we feel, because we can change what we think.

 Gave it a go? **Then give it a fist bump**.

Any thoughts about that conversation can be recorded here.

Parents, use this as a place to reflect on the conversation you had together:

Date of conversation . . . .

Home/school/significant events that are happening now

. . . .

How do you think it went?

. . . .

. . . .

What would you take from it?

. . . .

. . . .

Anything else you want to remember?

. . . .

. . . .

Compass Point 3: What Helps?

These conversations are all about sorting through the resources, tools and support that we have to hand (or could use) when times are tough. A chance to talk about challenging times and think about them in a different way.

Noticing there are ups as well as downs in life is important because it shows that difficult times pass. We also want to sort through the tools and support available that will help in getting through tough times.

What helps? Ups and Downs

This is a really simple conversation that is good for the 'all or nothing' thinkers. It helps us to hold on to the idea that some days are better than others, even if it's just by a smidge.

Some days are better than others and that's all we want from this conversation. If you have a bad day, the next one might be a bit better. This is important because when we go through a bad patch, we tend to see everything negatively and miss the moments that are better. This conversation is different to 'How are you? Mood Mountain' because it asks us to take a longer view and compare days.

What helps? Ups and Downs

This is a really simple conversation that is good for the 'all or nothing' thinkers. It helps us to hold on to the idea that some days are better than others, even if it's just by a smidge.

Conversation starters

- Let's think about the last few days...
  - Do a drawing for each day on the page to help remember which is which (say Monday is football practice, and so on). A week is a long time in politics and it's also true if you are 5 years old.
  - Now give each day a mark out of 10 (just say the numbers out loud if it's easier).
  - 10 out of 10 means it was a fantastic day, 0 out of 10 means it was a really, really bad day.

Sshh. Parents, don't say anything just yet...just watch and learn.

Keep talking

- Not all days are the same. Better days come after bad days. Let's say most days are 1/10, but one is 2/10. It's still low, but better than the others, so find out more about that day...
  - Something was a bit different on that day. What was it?
  - Why was it a bit better?
  - Can you do something to help push the number higher?
  - Can [insert family/friend name] do something to help?

If it feels too much, just discuss any two days and compare what is the same and what is different – job done.

What helps? Ups and Downs

This is a really simple conversation that is good for the 'all or nothing' thinkers. It helps us to hold on to the idea that some days are better than others, even if it's just by a smidge.

Feel incredible, when you bring this conversation to a close.

It might be hard work to think back over the last few days, so it's likely that most kids will need a break now. But if it feels like a good thing, they can record what they thought of this conversation here.

Parents, use this as a place to reflect on the conversation you had together:

Date of conversation . . . .

Home/school/significant events that are happening now

. . . .

How do you think it went?

. . . .

. . . .

What would you take from it?

. . . .

. . . .

Anything else you want to remember?

. . . .

. . . .

What helps? Really Rubbish

Talking about bad times we have had in life creates a bond between us. It also reminds us that we get through even really bad days – they will pass.

It might feel hard to talk about the worst times you have had in life, but these conversations are a chance to connect and to get 'in the pit' together (see Chapter 3 'Tough times? Climb into the pit with your child'). Even if you are talking about something that happened in the past, it is a bonding experience. Talking about the most challenging days is also important if we are to notice what helped us through, and remember that we got to better times.

If the worst day ever involves a family scene, it means you have enough trust in each other to share that. It's a chance to let each other know that talking about tough times is okay, which is a major part of lifelong wellbeing. It is also really encouraging because if we can talk about it, it means we don't have to act it out.

What helps? Really Rubbish

Talking about bad times we have had in life creates a bond between us. It also reminds us that we get through even really bad days – they will pass.

Conversation starters

- One of my worst days was [insert example].

- Tell me about one of the worst days you've ever had?

- You can draw it or write it on the picture.

Keep talking

- Who did you tell about it?

- What did you do or say to make yourself feel better?

- What did [insert family name/friend/teacher] do to help you?

- Now it's over, do you think about things in a different way ?

We are assuming that the rubbish time is in the past (or at least the worst part is over). If that's the case, it can be a brilliant symbolic exercise to draw or write the bad time on a piece of paper, scrunch it up or stamp on it, blow a raspberry at it (get creative) and put it in the bin. It's where rubbish belongs, after all.

You might even use your drawing on the picture page, but if there are heartfelt feelings on it, use another bit of paper. Bad times pass, so show them the door.

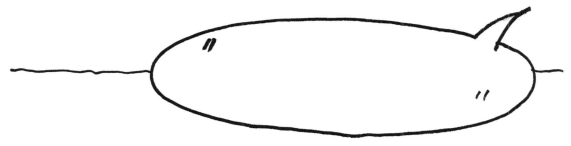

What helps? Really Rubbish

Talking about bad times we have had in life creates a bond between us. It also reminds us that we get through even really bad days – they will pass.

It's a fine compliment if someone shares their troubles with you. **Fist bump this** and end the conversation feeling good about what you have shared.

This might be quite an emotional conversation, so suggest that kids take a break (once you have marked it with your ritual together). Some kids, however, may want to hang around with you, particularly if they have shared something major, so if they feel up to it, invite them to write or draw their thoughts about the conversation here.

Parents, use this as a place to reflect on the conversation you had together:

Date of conversation . . . .

Home/school/significant events that are happening now

. . . .

How do you think it went?

. . . .

. . . .

What would you take from it?

. . . .

. . . .

Anything else you want to remember?

. . . .

. . . .

What helps? Support Squad

This conversation is about figuring out the VIPs in a child's life – particularly trusted adults and friends. It highlights social support, safety nets and friendships.

This is a conversation about noticing the Very Important People (VIPs) in our world. These people are likely to be the same people who would support us when things are hard. They may be family members, or they may be friends, teachers or any significant others. Sometimes, teddies, pets, or loved ones who are no longer around (for example, grandparents) are included because they are important too. The order of description can be meaningful, so watch and learn from it. This is a chance to map out the people in our world and bank it for a rainy day.

Very young children are often more likely to name people that they see frequently in their daily routine, because they tend to be more 'in the moment'. As children get older, they may also hold someone in mind who they may not see day to day.

What helps? Support Squad

This conversation is about figuring out the VIPs in a child's life – particularly trusted adults and friends. It highlights social support, safety nets and friendships.

Conversation starters

- Choose a good colour and draw or write something as a reminder that the person at the top of the pyramid pile is YOU.

- Let's try and think of the important people in your life. Write/draw them on the page.

- Think about people at home and school, family, friends or anyone else.

- You can add more people (or pets or toys) if you like.

Keep talking

- Put a circle around someone who you could tell if you had a big worry. Choose one who lives with you and another who lives somewhere else.

Ideally find at least one trusted adult at home **and** one outside home. If there are no obvious candidates in the picture, parents may want to suggest an appropriate person such as a favourite teacher and add their name/picture, and see if the child accepts this suggestion.

SUPPORT
SQUAD

What helps? Support Squad

This conversation is about figuring out the VIPs in a child's life – particularly trusted adults and friends. It highlights social support, safety nets and friendships.

End this conversation by counting together the number of people/pets/cuddly toys listed. Counting them up is gratifying because it says, in many different ways, that you have people on your side. It also underlies the investment of time taken making the picture, and we all know how good it feels when someone notices our hard work.

If kids want to record what they thought of this conversation, they can draw or write it here (most will have had enough by now, so don't force it).

Parents, use this as a place to reflect on the conversation you had together:

Date of conversation . . . .

Home/school/significant events that are happening now

. . . .

How do you think it went?

. . . .

. . . .

What would you take from it?

. . . .

. . . .

Anything else you want to remember?

. . . .

. . . .

What helps? Helping Hands

A discussion about what the VIPs in our life can say on the one hand, or do on the other hand, to help us through a difficult time.

In 'What helps? Support Squad', we pinned down a list of Very Important People. In this conversation, we take it a step further and think about **how** our people might help when things are rough. It might include the people in Support Squad, or maybe there are others that spring to mind here. The more the merrier when it comes to having a team on your side.

What helps? Helping Hands

A discussion about what the VIPs in our life can say on the one hand, or do on the other hand, to help us through a difficult time.

Conversation starters

- Think about a time that was hard (maybe use 'What helps? Really Rubbish') or pick something else (for example, when you worried about a school test, or had a row with friends) that happened in the last few weeks.

- Tell me about it...

- Pick someone who helped you sort out that trouble, and draw or write their name inside one of the circles in the picture.

- Think for a minute about what the person **said** or **did** (or maybe both) and draw or write that in the hand holding that circle.

Keep talking

- Telling an adult you trust about a bad time ALWAYS helps – is that true?

- Was there anything that your Support Squad tried (because they care about you) but that didn't help so much?

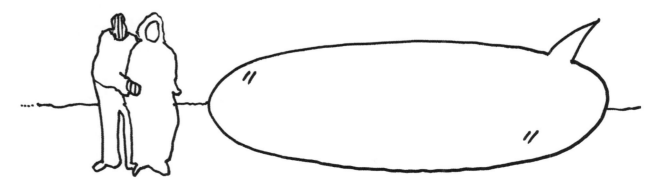

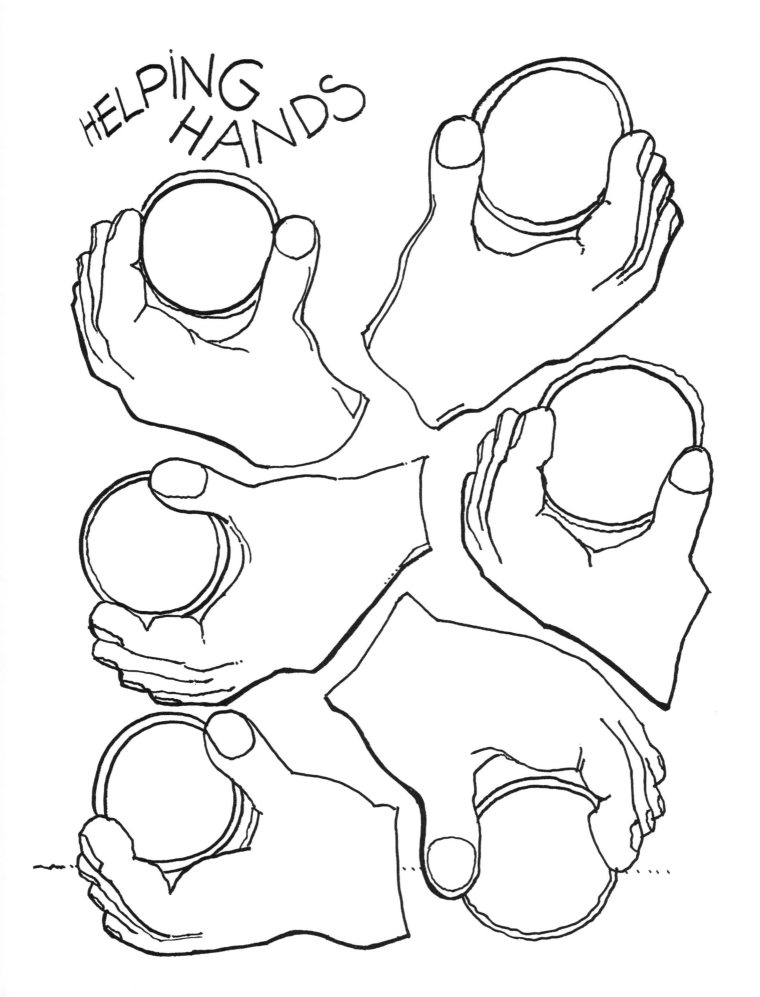

What helps? Helping Hands

A discussion about what the VIPs in our life can say on the one hand, or do on the other hand, to help us through a difficult time.

No answers? No problem. Just listening is a triumph. If you managed that, we salute you. **Fist bump and feel good** so your kids will come back and talk again and again.

Any comments about this one can be written or drawn here (but only if kids are keen to do so).

Parents, use this as a place to reflect on the conversation you had together:

Date of conversation . . . .

Home/school/significant events that are happening now

. . . .

How do you think it went?

. . . .

. . . .

What would you take from it?

. . . .

. . . .

Anything else you want to remember?

. . . .

. . . .

What helps? Stepping Stones

It's important to use our support network, but it's empowering to remember we can help ourselves too, so spend time talking through self-help superpowers.

It is really important to lean on others for help when you are in trouble – and always a good idea for children to tell a trusted adult. But having ways to manage a challenge using our own self-help superpowers just gives us more options. Not all of the ideas will work and some might feel good for a minute or two but aren't **really** sorting out the problem (like hiding under your duvet when there is a school test). Sometimes you can only find out what works by giving it a go. It's the best way to learn.

What helps? Stepping Stones

It's important to use our support network, but it's empowering to remember we can help ourselves too, so spend time talking through self-help superpowers.

Conversation starters

- Look at the picture. Write or draw something to stand for a 'tough time' you've had on the river bank.
- Now let's think about the things that you said or did that helped you over to the other side onto the 'better times' side of the river.
- Use a stepping stone to write or draw each thing that you did to help yourself.

Shhh. Parents, don't say anything yet...

If you need some prompts to get going, try these:

- Did you tell yourself something that helped? Maybe you have a good saying?
- What about telling other people about your trouble?
- Did you ask for help?
- Did you do some exercise to feel better?
- What about something to take your mind off it? (See 'Who are you? Memory Frame Game'.)

Keep talking

- Maybe you looked back and thought about another time like this? What did you do then?
- What are your top tips for managing hard days?
- Have you spotted the shark fins? Yikes! Draw on a shark fin something you have tried that didn't help.

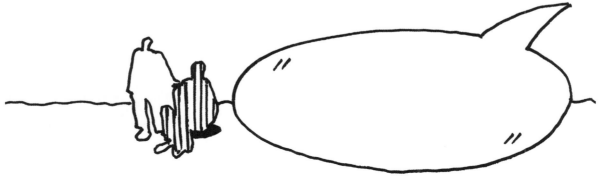

What helps? Stepping Stones

It's important to use our support network, but it's empowering to remember we can help ourselves too, so spend time talking through self-help superpowers.

Sharing often takes courage. Listening often takes strength. Both get first prize from us. Mark it together now.

Many kids will need to have a change of scene after this conversation – there is a lot to think about, after all. So, suggest a different activity, but if there are comments from kids, write or draw them here.

Parents, use this as a place to reflect on the conversation you had together:

Date of conversation . . . .

Home/school/significant events that are happening now

. . . .

How do you think it went?

. . . .

. . . .

What would you take from it?

. . . .

. . . .

Anything else you want to remember?

. . . .

. . . .

What helps? Power Up

Talking about how stress helps us to figure out how to manage it and how it can actually help us. It's all a question of how you see it. One of the authors' favourite conversations, this is great for kids who get overwhelmed with stress.

Stress doesn't have to be a bad thing – in fact, a quick burst of stress can power us on. The way we think about stress changes its effect on our brain and body. If we remind ourselves that it is extra energy to boost our performance, then our brain reacts in a better way.

This is a family challenge since parents influence their children's ideas. If parents can think about a quick burst of stress as energizing, then their children will too. In the moment, we can describe that racing heart and churning tummy as extra energy to help meet the challenge in front of us. Keep this mindset and then when you face a new challenge, your brain will actually grow with all the benefits that a burst of stress can bring.

What helps? Power Up

Talking about how stress helps us to figure out how to manage it and how it can actually help us. It's all a question of how you see it. One of the authors' favourite conversations, this is great for kids who get overwhelmed with stress.

Psst ... This conversation has an 'AHA' moment, so try to get to the end if you can.

Conversation starters

- If you put batteries in the wrong way around, they don't work and the energy drains straight out of them. But if you put those same batteries in the right way around, they totally power up. Remember this... We are coming back to it.

- When we have a challenge (for example, reading out loud in front of the class or going on stage), our brain sends a message to our body saying 'Get ready'.

- How does your body react? Think about your head, hands, heart, tummy, skin, the inside of your mouth.

- Draw your nervous feelings, using Nega-steve in the picture. His batteries are in the wrong way around and he is feeling pretty drained.

Keep talking

- Do you know the 'Stress Secret'? A quick burst of stress is actually an ENERGY boost, so your body is ready for **any** challenge. (Hardly anyone knows that.)

- Draw the **same nervous feelings** but use Posy-tive's figure this time.

- Posy-tive's feelings are just the same as Nega-steve's, but **her** batteries are the right way up because she knows the secret. She is energized and raring to go.

- Think about a time when you were really excited. What happened to your body then? How are stressed and excited the same/different?

- Maybe you DID know the secret ?

What helps? Power Up

Talking about how stress helps us to figure out how to manage it and how it can actually help us. It's all a question of how you see it. One of the authors' favourite conversations, this is great for kids who get overwhelmed with stress.

Finish positively – all's well that ends well, after all.

Most kids will want to do something else now, but if there are any burning thoughts or comments about this conversation, jot them down or draw them here.

Parents, use this as a place to reflect on the conversation you had together:

Date of conversation . . . .

Home/school/significant events that are happening now

. . . .

How do you think it went?

. . . .

. . . .

What would you take from it?

. . . .

. . . .

Anything else you want to remember?

. . . .

. . . .

Compass Point 4: What Gets in the Way?

To some degree these are the most challenging conversations because they focus on areas that get in the way of our lives, but they are an important part of family conversation. This is a supported, structured and gentle start to exploring obstacles and ways around them.

This is not about pointing out *each others'* mistakes. This is an invitation to reflect *on ourselves*, ask what gets in our way and maybe think about what we would like to do differently. It's the beginning of a long-term, possibly lifelong project.

These sorts of discussions are very much part of healthy relationship building, but if your family or your relationship is feeling a bit vulnerable at the moment, you may want to come back to this section later.

What gets in the way? Oops Loops

This conversation is about the moments when we think to ourselves, 'Oops, that didn't go well.' Doing this when we are calm means we can think it through and talk it over.

See this as a chance to test out what happens when you share at home stuff that went wrong. The **priority** here is about practising sharing when things don't go well or there is a mess-up, so try not to fixate on fixing it. It's best to use recent examples but make sure the moment has passed – talking about events in the past brings down the emotional temperature of a discussion and means you can reflect on things in a different way. We know this because brain science has told us so (see Chapter 3, 'Calm brains work best'). Whether you are a child or an adult, it is very hard to use the self-reflection part of the brain (the **frontal cortex**, for fact nerds) when we are fearful or angry. The beauty of this conversation is that you can talk about an issue when you are **both** feeling calm and so you are able to think it through. You have space to be genuinely interested in why something happened, which is almost impossible to do in the heat of the moment.

If there are any 'Oops' moments that children spot by themselves (and not because an adult mentioned them), it is very valuable, particularly in younger children. Being able to do that is a sign of a well-rounded young person in the making. These sorts of events are worth much praise and discussion because you have struck (self-regulation) gold.

What gets in the way? Oops Loops

This conversation is about the moments when we think to ourselves, 'Oops, that didn't go well.' Doing this when we are calm means we can think it through and talk it over.

 ## Conversation starters

- We all mess up now and again. I messed up by [insert example].

- This is a rollercoaster. Some bits are high (the good bits in your week). The low loops are the 'Oops' moments.

- Think about the last few days. Were there any times when you thought, 'Oops, that was a mistake' (for example, having a strop or maybe avoiding something)?

- Draw or write these in the rollercoaster car at the bottom of the loop in the picture.

- Let's also remember the moments when you thought, 'Good for me.' Do a drawing or write that in the car at the top of the loop.

 ## Keep talking

- Does that 'Oops' happen a lot? (For example, are rows frequent or worries common?)

- What was happening just before your 'Oops' moment?

- Do you have any ideas about why it turned out that way?

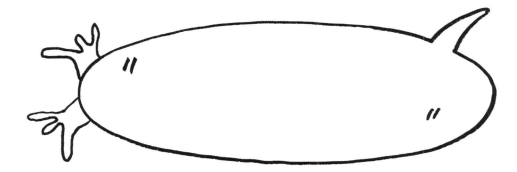

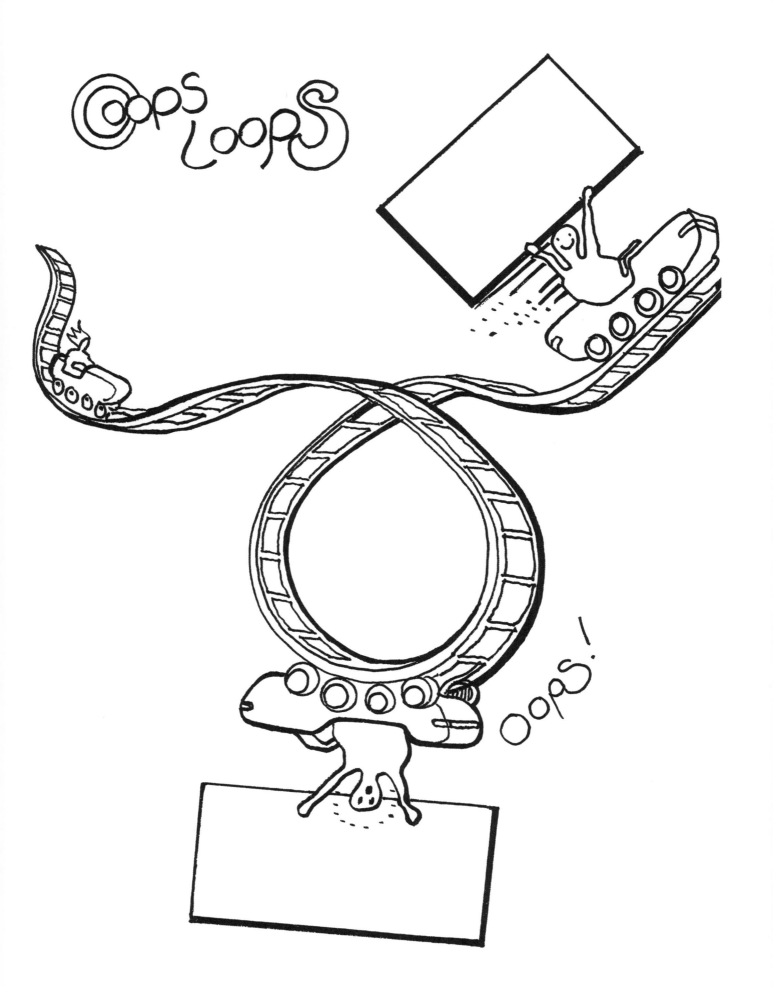

What gets in the way? Oops Loops

This conversation is about the moments when we think to ourselves, 'Oops, that didn't go well.' Doing this when we are calm means we can think it through and talk it over.

Talking together about a mistake, is a win. Celebrate it.

After a conversation, most kids will need a break, but if they want to remember something about this conversation before they shoot off, here is the place to note or draw it.

Parents, use this as a place to reflect on the conversation you had together:

Date of conversation . . . .

Home/school/significant events that are happening now

. . . .

How do you think it went?

. . . .

. . . .

What would you take from it?

. . . .

. . . .

Anything else you want to remember?

. . . .

. . . .

What gets in the way? Muddle and Make Up

Discussing a time when family life got in a muddle (like a row) and figuring out – after the storm has passed – how it got sorted, is healing. If your family find arguments get in the way a lot, this one is for you.

Remember that darned sock from Chapter 2? Knowing that rows happen even in a healthy, loving relationship is part of a relationship skill set (though if it's the same row over and over, it can mean you are a bit stuck). It's okay to disagree. Finding a way to make up after a row is also part of the good relationship toolkit. Let's say homework time is an utter stress-fest for your family. Everyone dreads it, and it always ends in a row. Have this conversation at a time when homework is **not** on the agenda and shake off your expectations. If you can do **that**, you might open up a whole new world of homework harmony.

Try really, really hard to let one another speak without interrupting. If that's difficult in your family, try the 'chat hat' technique. You can only talk if you are wearing the 'chat hat'. If you want to speak while the other person is talking, raise your hand and your partner will pass you the hat. (You could use any household object, obviously.)

This conversation can be a right old button-presser. Parents, be particularly aware of this, as the grown-ups in the room. We absolutely ban saying, 'I only do that because you...' But you can say 'Thank you for telling me' (or similar) as much as you like.

What gets in the way? Muddle and Make Up

Discussing a time when family life got in a muddle (like a row) and figuring out – after the storm has passed – how it got sorted, is healing. If your family find arguments get in the way a lot, this one is for you.

Conversation starters

Pick a time you got in a muddle and had a row. Maybe it was about coming off devices or bedtimes. (If children pick the muddle, motivation for the conversation will be higher.)

- Step 1: Who was there? (Draw/write their names.)
- Step 2: Draw something to stand for the muddle.
  - What happened just **before** the muddle happened?
  - Where were you? What time was it?
  - What happened next?
  - How did it end?
- Step 3: Make up.
  - What did [name] do or say to make up?
  - What did you do or say to make up?

Keep talking

- What tips could you give me so that the muddle doesn't happen again?
- What tips do you think I would give **you**?

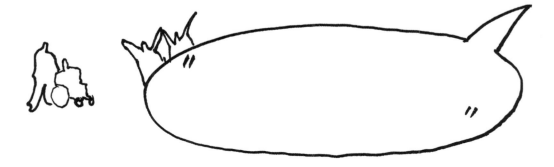

MUDDLE AND MAKE-UP

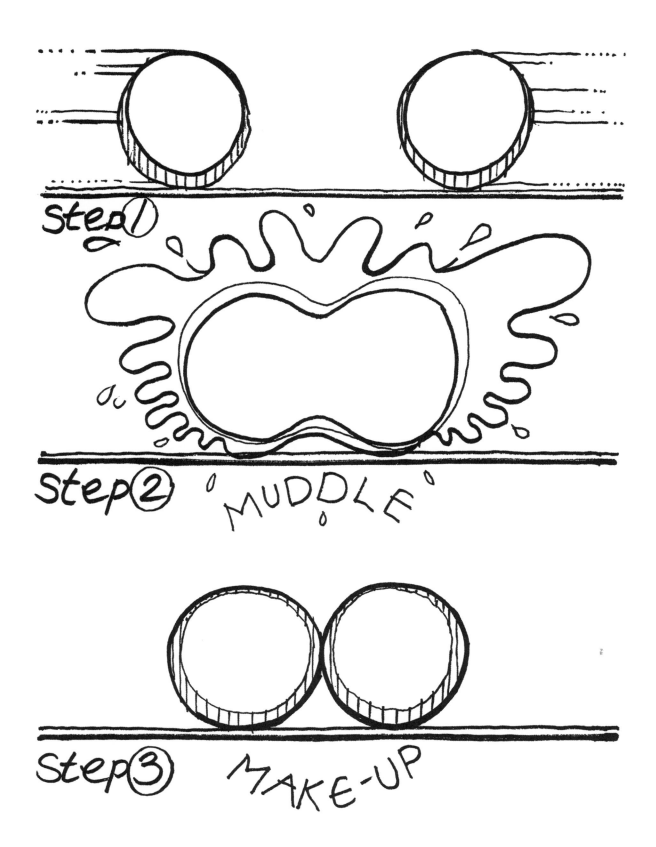

What gets in the way? Muddle and Make Up

Discussing a time when family life got in a muddle (like a row) and figuring out – after the storm has passed – how it got sorted, is healing. If your family find arguments get in the way a lot, this one is for you.

 If emotions run a bit high, maybe you are still in the middle of the muddle. Park it (celebrate that smart choice) and come back to it another day.

Be gentle with each other during this conversation. It's particularly important to end with a positive. Try this: tell each other your favourite thing about one another. (This utterly transforms the atmosphere, when otherwise you might want to cheerfully throttle each other.)

Suggest a change of activity now for your child, but before they go, they might want to give this conversation a comment (or a thumbs up/down). Here is the place to draw or write that.

Parents, use this as a place to reflect on the conversation you had together:

Date of conversation . . . .

Home/school/significant events that are happening now

. . . .

How do you think it went?

. . . .

. . . .

What would you take from it?

. . . .

. . . .

Anything else you want to remember?

. . . .

. . . .

What gets in the way? What If-ing

A conversation about sorting through concerns, to figure out what is useful and what is big, heavy, old baggage weighing you down. Worriers will get a lot out of this one.

For some people, the biggest barrier to moving forward is anxiety. Worries are a very powerful set of brakes, keeping you stuck in one place (and can sometimes make you roll backwards). What if-ing goes something like this: 'What if a lion eats me on the way to school?' or 'What if I'm not good enough?' and is almost always 'just worry'. (By saying 'just worry', we are not dismissing how difficult it is to boss back a worry, but instead making the point that it is **only** worry that is standing in the way and not anything else.) Worrying doesn't make the world any safer, but it means you miss out on things or feel horrible before you take the plunge anyway. If you are the sort of person who worries, it's important not to talk yourself out of an interesting experience for example, or a new friendship, because 'what if' worries got in the way. The trick is figuring out the difference between sensible thinking through of the pros and cons (recommended) and keeping that separate from 'what if-ing' (not recommended).

We all have our own brand of worry. If it's getting in the way, it must feel serious, so it's important to respect another's worry, even if it doesn't make any sense to you.

What gets in the way? What If-ing

A conversation about sorting through concerns, to figure out what is useful and what is big, heavy, old baggage weighing you down. Worriers will get a lot out of this one.

Conversation starters

- This is what if-ing: 'What if I get the worst mark in the class?' 'What if a dog bites me in the park?' What if-ing weighs us down and gets in the way.

- Draw some of your 'what if' worries in the sack in the picture. If you draw a little bag, it's a little worry. If it's a bigger bag, it is a bigger worry.

- Choose one worry bag and let's imagine for a minute that it really **did** happen. What was the worst bit? (Sometimes we realize we could cope if we think it through to the 'bottom line' of that worry. Result? The worry has lost its power.)

Keep talking

- Let's sort out what we might do if this worry actually did happen.

- Have a look at 'What helps: Stepping Stones' and tell me your self-help superpowers.

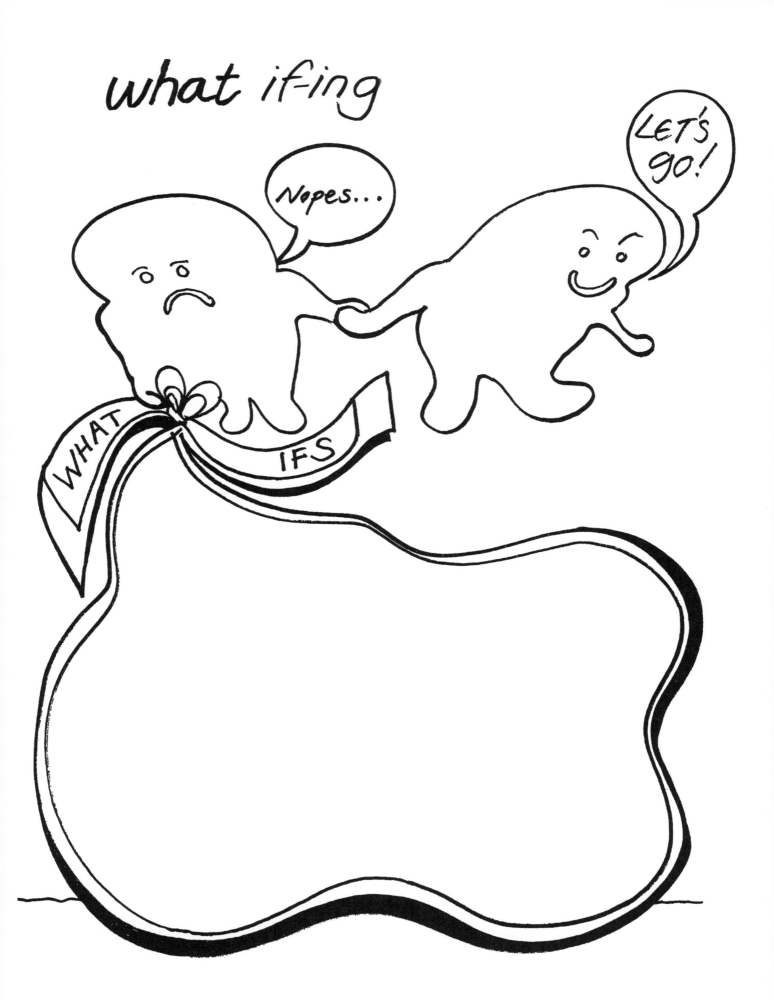

What gets in the way? What If-ing

A conversation about sorting through concerns, to figure out what is useful and what is big, heavy, old baggage weighing you down. Worriers will get a lot out of this one.

Sharing worries can make us feel vulnerable, so a shout out to you if you were able to share.

If children have said something that makes them particularly vulnerable, they might want to stick by you. So, invite them to write or draw what they thought of this conversation here. (Other kids may be ready to go off and do something else.)

Parents, use this as a place to reflect on the conversation you had together:

Date of conversation . . . .

Home/school/significant events that are happening now

. . . .

How do you think it went?

. . . .

. . . .

What would you take from it?

. . . .

. . . .

Anything else you want to remember?

. . . .

. . . .

What gets in the way? Uh-oh...Spoiler Alert

Talking about our meltdowns is less threatening if we describe them as separate from us – a bit like a 'baddie' who spoils things. Creative kids will love this one.

Getting in a rage happens to us all sometimes, but we know this sort of thing happens more often in younger children and is a bit more common in boys. There can be lots of reasons why people act in this way. Sometimes it's because of misunderstandings between people, sometimes it's because someone might act before thinking, sometimes it's actually worry 'in disguise', but it comes out as if that person is cross or mad. Sometimes it's a combination of all three. The picture below is a good reminder about some of the complicated feelings behind expressed anger. Separating the problem (a rage) from the person is a tried and tested technique that frees up **everyone** in the family to get creative about solutions.

What gets in the way? Uh-oh...Spoiler Alert

Talking about our meltdowns is less threatening if we describe them as separate from us – a bit like a 'baddie' who spoils things. Creative kids will love this one.

Conversation starters

- We all get into strops sometimes, but if it's happening a lot, it might spoil fun times with family or friends.
- First, we are going to give the strop a name. Kids sometimes use names such as 'The Big Red Rage' or 'Meltdown Marvin', but you can call it anything you like. [One child we worked with was a Chelsea football fan. He hated his rages so much that he named them 'Tottenham Hotspur', Chelsea's biggest rival. Genius.]
- Now draw [insert name] in the doorway. It can be a colour or a shape or it can even look like a person.
- How would we know [insert name] has arrived?

Keep talking

- Sometimes [insert name] sneaks in and no one notices at first. At other times they come crashing through the door. What are the 'door-step' signs? Draw or write them on the door.
- What do you do when [insert name] is in the room?
- Where can you feel it in your body?
- What are you thinking to yourself when [insert name] arrives?
- We all want [insert name] to quit spoiling things. What can we all do together to get them back out of the room?

Spoiler Alert challenge: This is an exercise we use routinely to help families spot a potential emotional meltdown. Some families may choose to do it. It's not strictly speaking part of the conversation but good practice to generalize the principles in the conversation to day-to-day life. A prize goes to the family member who can spot when Meltdown Marvin [or chosen name] came into the room. To win, you have to be the first one to say the name out loud.

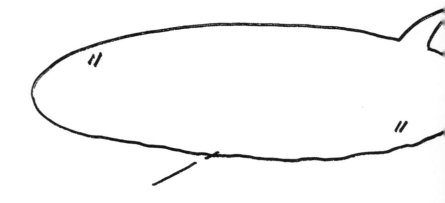

What gets in the way? Uh-oh...Spoiler Alert

Talking about our meltdowns is less threatening if we describe them as separate from us – a bit like a 'baddie' who spoils things. Creative kids will love this one.

It takes particular courage to discuss our own meltdowns because this is often considered 'a problem' in a way that other difficulties are not (for example, sleepless nights). For those who tend to get into rages, it is a chance to feel proud because they are taking a step forward by **talking** about it. So, parents, treat it like the golden opportunity that it is, and heap well-deserved praise on a child who tries to talk about their tricky moments, rather than acting them out. **Fist bump it**.

Have a break now but if there are any comments about this conversation, kids could write or draw them here.

Parents, use this as a place to reflect on the conversation you had together:

Date of conversation . . . .

Home/school/significant events that are happening now

. . . .

How do you think it went?

. . . .

. . . .

What would you take from it?

. . . .

. . . .

Anything else you want to remember?

. . . .

. . . .

What gets in the way? Road Blocks

There is no such thing as a bad idea when it comes to figuring out how to shift obstacles in the way of a shared family goal. This is a wonderful conversation to develop problem-solving skills and to encourage speaking up in your community.

Sometimes, little changes can make a big difference and make life easier. If we keep a growth mindset (see Chapter 2), we are much more likely to move forward from mistakes, because we believe that they are a valuable part of learning. Bring mistakes home and discuss them together without judgement. Sift through them for clues that help change things for the better. Let's say our goal is one morning (just one) getting ready for school and work without a family row. Think through what gets in the way, and how to remove those road blocks to get closer to the destination goal. Some ideas you try won't work. Some might even make the row bigger, but this information moves things along too. Warning: DO NOT have this conversation if you are all still simmering from a morning row – remember that calm brains communicate best (see Chapter 3).

Any suggestion is worth exploring. A suggestion which may seem unlikely to help at first, is important to try for a number of reasons. First, it might work. Second, it shows everyone's ideas are valuable in the family (and remember how important this is, see the page in the Introduction and Example Conversations, when we introduce the speech bubbles). Third, we are all much more likely to persist with an approach that we have thought up ourselves.

What gets in the way? Road Blocks

There is no such thing as a bad idea when it comes to figuring out how to shift obstacles in the way of a shared family goal. This is a wonderful conversation to develop problem-solving skills and to encourage speaking up in your community.

Conversation starters

- Let's choose a family goal as our destination. (Word it positively: 'a calm morning' rather than 'no rows'.) Draw/write it in the sunrise on the picture.

- We are at the beginning of the road. Let's think about the road blocks in the way. Draw/write the things that get in the way on the blocks (for example, car keys go missing or school books are spread all over the house).

Keep talking

- There are lots of different ways to get past a road block. You could push it, pull it or climb right over it. So, there could be lots of different ideas that might work and you still get to same destination.

- Look at each road block and let's think what could we do about it? For example, everyone could pack their schoolbag the night before (and before screen time to increase motivation ...Ahem). Let's put our ideas in the ideas tool box here by the side of the road.

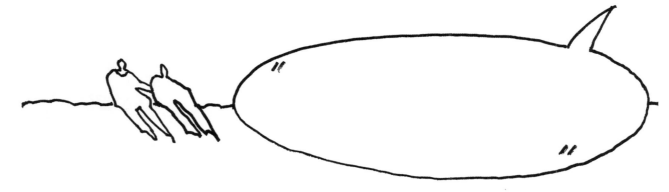

What gets in the way? Road Blocks

There is no such thing as a bad idea when it comes to figuring out how to shift obstacles in the way of a shared family goal. This is a wonderful conversation to develop problem-solving skills and to encourage speaking up in your community.

The **most** important point here is that you are sowing the seeds of a strong and successful relationship. Think about it: you talked about a tricky time together, looked at the problems together and **maybe** came up with a way forward together. Congratulations to you both.

Kids might write or draw their ideas here but otherwise, stop there and leave feeling good.

Parents, use this as a place to reflect on the conversation you had together:

Date of conversation . . . .

Home/school/significant events that are happening now

. . . .

How do you think it went?

. . . .

. . . .

What would you take from it?

. . . .

. . . .

Anything else you want to remember?

. . . .

. . . .

Pick 'n' Mix

Communication is a two-way process, so this is a chance to mix it up a bit. Pick any one of the conversations and swap roles so that, this time, parents share *their* thoughts and feelings, and children listen. This is a great way to develop empathy.

Children are in the driving seat this time. Communication is a two-way street after all and it's a good idea in any relationship to see things from someone else's point of view. It can be a revelation to children that their parents have an emotional life. We suggest that children might pick one or two of the conversations, and ask parents about *their* ideas, memories or feelings. This is your time to shine as a parent and model all the listening and sharing skills that we hope children will develop as they grow up.

Remember that parents are the grown-ups and because they are in charge it might change what is shared or how things are said. However, the essence of sharing good times and bad, emotions, memories and dreams is the same.

Younger children will not be able to read the conversation starters, but they may remember the gist of the exercise if they have had that conversation before. Slightly older children may need a little reading help from grown-ups.

Children may come up with their own approach, which is much more interesting than using someone else's. If that's the case, go for it, if that works for you both.

Just remember to Finish Feeling Fabulous.

Last Word

Well, there it is.

We sincerely hope that this is the start of a journey to stronger and healthier family relationships. The ideas and feelings you shared are precious, of course, but exploring the *idea* of conversation together is just as valuable. Children will know for sure that conversation is high on the family agenda because they have *experienced it* with you. It will significantly increase the chances that even the least talkative of children will take the chance to engage in conversation in the future. Saying to your kids, 'You can always talk to me,' is one thing, but using this book and *doing it* together is something altogether more powerful. It means the message will stick.

If talking has been hard at times, it will get easier with practice, so don't give up, just **ASKE**:

- *Anything goes.* Nothing is off the table. Sharing something doesn't mean agreeing with it.
- *Shhh.* Leave space to listen, and show caring by just staying alongside your child.
- *Keep talking.* Don't worry if there is no response at first – try again later.
- *End positively.* If we feel good doing something, we want to do it again.

Here's to a life-time of *Incredible Conversations* together.

We would take it as a great compliment if this book becomes redundant after a while because you are making up your own *Incredible Conversations*. Start now.

Boom! You've just had an *Incredible Conversation*.

Appendix 1

Example Conversations

These conversations between parents and children, reproduced with kind permission, might help if you are feeling stuck or perhaps need to inspire a reticent participant. We have included a selection of conversations and a range of ages and family contexts. You will see that there is no 'right' way to approach these conversations; if it gets you talking then our job is done.

The examples are reproduced in black and white, but we would strongly encourage using different colours because it can really help express ideas in a creative way.

In each description, we reference relevant issues that we have raised in Part 1 to help you see how the mindset techniques we describe will come to life as you learn to use these Incredible Conversations together.

Who are you? My Best Day

An easy start, usually fun and full of positivity – a way of finding out about people, places and things that are loved or wished for.

Alfie and Sam – My Best Day

Alfie is 11 years old and utterly charming. He's a brilliant footballer and loves gaming. He's dyslexic. For some neurodiverse kids, any pen and paper activities may have negative associations (see 'Top Tips: A reluctant participant? Any bad associations with a paper and pen?'). When his mum, Sam, told him about Incredible Conversations, he said 'I wasn't sure…I thought it was going to be a bit like homework…but it was much fun-er.' His favourite conversation was My Best Day. 'It was really good…the conversations make me feel good about myself…and anyone can do them!'

Sam said she thought she might have to read up and 'get more prepared' before trying the conversations but was surprised to find it felt really natural. The family do a lot of socializing together and have strong communication skills but even so, she was delighted to find out new ideas about Alfie's hopes and dreams: 'his answers made me smile,' she added. They sometimes use the conversations at bedtime because that works well for their routine. She added that Alfie has been pestering her to do more conversations, so despite Alfie's initial reservations, Incredible Conversations work for Team Alfie.

Who are you? Think of a Link

A conversation about similarities (and differences) between family and others in our world – ideas about who we are or what we could become often pop up.
Dara and Carol – Think of a Link

Dara is 9 and has recently been placed in foster care with carer, Carol. Dara is a thoughtful child who loves music but is nervous and tends to be wary of getting it wrong. He has had a lot of loss in the past. Carol is an experienced carer and wanted to get to know him better and build bonds with him, so she suggested they start with Think of a Link. In many situations it might be a good idea to ask your child to choose the conversation because it can increase children's motivation; however, because of Dara's specific situation, Carol steered him to this particular conversation (see 'Top Tips: These conversations could form a life story book for looked-after children').

He was reticent to say anything at all, at first. But Carol, very wisely waited and said gently 'Just have a go when you are ready'. After some time, Dara offered that he and his (biological) mum both liked sushi, and then with a lot of praise from Carol, he began to add some more links. Right at the end, Dara pointed out some differences and said that he celebrated different holidays from his foster family. He didn't write this down which is okay of course – this is a conversation, not a worksheet, after all. Carol said it was a good sign he talked about differences because it might be a sign he felt safe enough to offer personal information (see 'Anything goes' in the Introduction). Although Carol was already aware of his family traditions, she wanted him to feel encouraged to share anything. 'He loved the Boom! fist bump at the end' Carol commented. Because of his early experiences, learning that it is okay to speak up will take some time, but Carol has helped him start his journey (see 'Top Tips: It takes time to learn new habits, especially if the old routines were stressful').

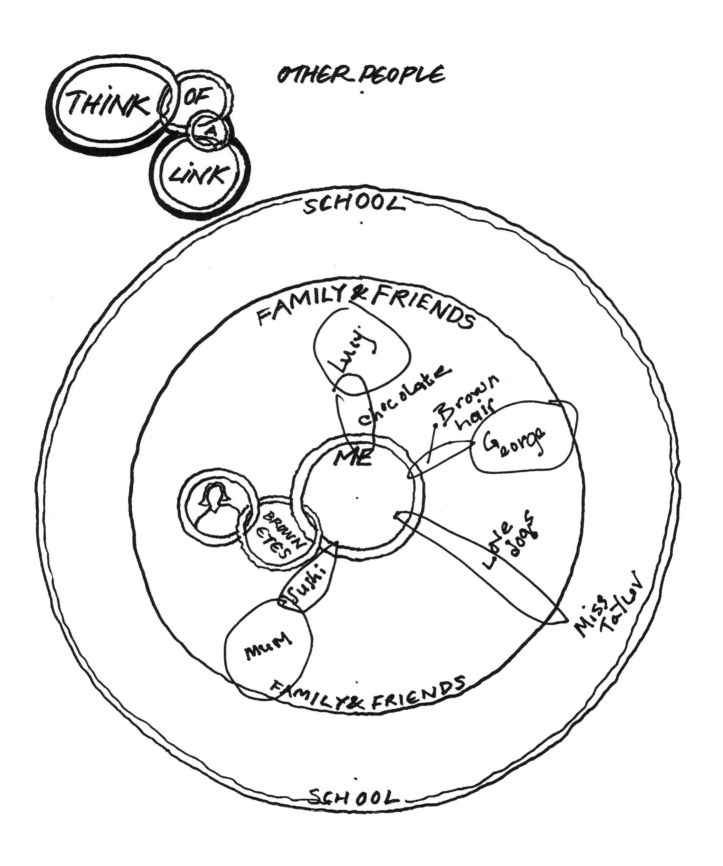

THINK OF A LINK

OTHER PEOPLE

SCHOOL

FAMILY & FRIENDS

Lucy

chocolate

Brown hair

George

ME

BROWN EYES

Love dogs

Miss Tatlin

Sushi

MUM

FAMILY & FRIENDS

SCHOOL

OTHER PEOPLE

Who are you? Memory Frame Game

A focus on the good old times. Talking about a favourite memory is a great bonding experience and can be a superb distraction for worriers.

Elliot and Peter – The Memory Frame Game

At 10 years old, Elliot is an Incredible creator with an eye for design that many adults would envy. He has a passion for marine biology. His mum died when he was a toddler and although he and his dad, Peter, talk often about his mum with warmth, humour and sensitivity, the Memory Frame Game could have potentially raised some hard emotions for the family. Elliot chose a scene from a family holiday that made him laugh, 'It was really fun (to do)' he said. The memory Elliot chose was not the one that Peter thought he might pick and this insightful reflection highlights why it's a good idea to stay curious during conversations with your child because you never know what you might find out if you keep an open mind (see 'How to use this book: Who are you?' in the Introduction). It is testament to Peter that he went, without question, with Elliot's idea because letting your child set the agenda in conversations (at least sometimes) is validating for them and will vastly increase the chances of more meaningful conversations happening in the family (see 'How to use this book: Who are you?' in the Introduction).

Elliot thought doing the conversations made him 'think about things differently'. This sort of comment from a young person is inspiring to hear because we know that talking out loud with someone we trust, evolves our thinking about our own opinions, emotions and self-knowledge. As Daniel Seigel said, conversation is a 'sorting space' for ideas (see Chapter 3, 'Top Tips: Asking about a problem won't create a problem'). Peter added, 'It was a wonderful way to connect with Elliot – unlocking feelings without drama.'

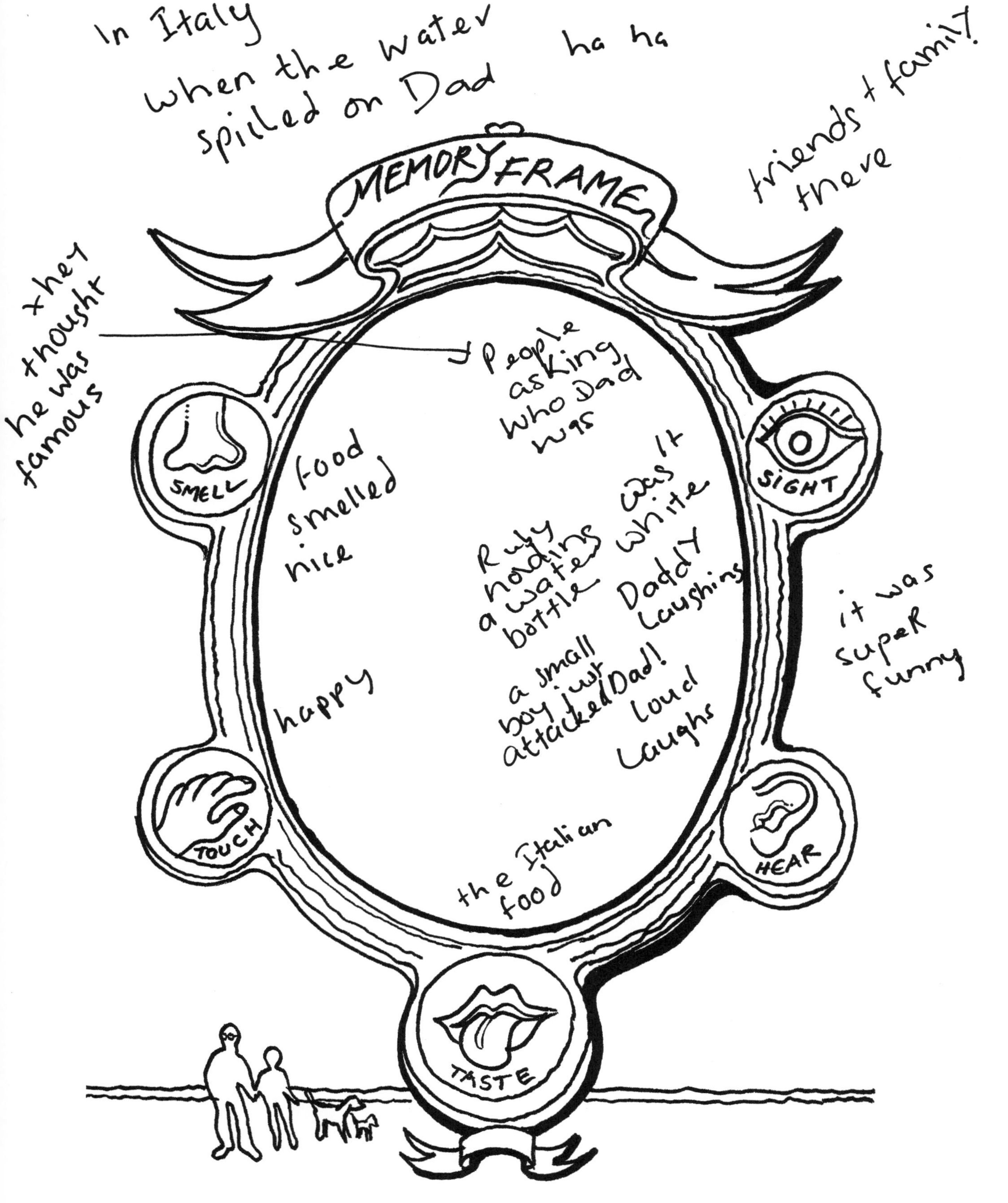

In Italy
When the water
spilled on Dad   ha ha

friends + family
there

MEMORY FRAME

they
thought
he was
famous

People
asking
Who Dad
was

SMELL

SIGHT

food
smelled
nice

Ruby
holding
a water
bottle

it
was
white

Daddy
Laughing

a small
boy just
attacked Dad!
Loud
Laughs

happy

it was
super
funny

TOUCH

HEAR

the Italian
food

TASTE

How are you? Mood Mountain

Sometimes it's hard to describe how you feel. This is an easy way to describe where you are at today, without saying a word.

Yasmin and Darius – Mood Mountain

Yasmin is 10, delights in singing and is a big cricket fan like her dad. She liked the look of Mood Mountain, so her dad, Darius, went with her choice and they made a den with sofa cushions where they talked and drew. He wrote down her words, which often works well. He said, 'I think the novelty of talking in the den sparked her interest' (see 'Top Tips: This is not homework, so don't make it feel like it is'). He added that in some ways he felt cautious about this conversation because he'd never thought to ask her about her mood day to day and wondered what she might say. This is a common concern (see 'Top Tips: Asking about a problem won't create a problem').

Yasmin said she liked hearing about 'Dad's day on the summit' best (he chose the day she was born). Darius commented that hearing about the time when she felt at her worst in the pit (when her party was cancelled during lockdown) was difficult to hear but he listened and wrote down what she said. Writing your child's words gives them some importance which validates the ideas, (See 'An accessible layout designed for you both' in the Introduction). After a bit, they went on to talk about her 11th birthday plans. They decided to make their own ritual to mark the end of their conversation which was – you guessed it – a song that Yasmin made up. A star is born, Yasmin.

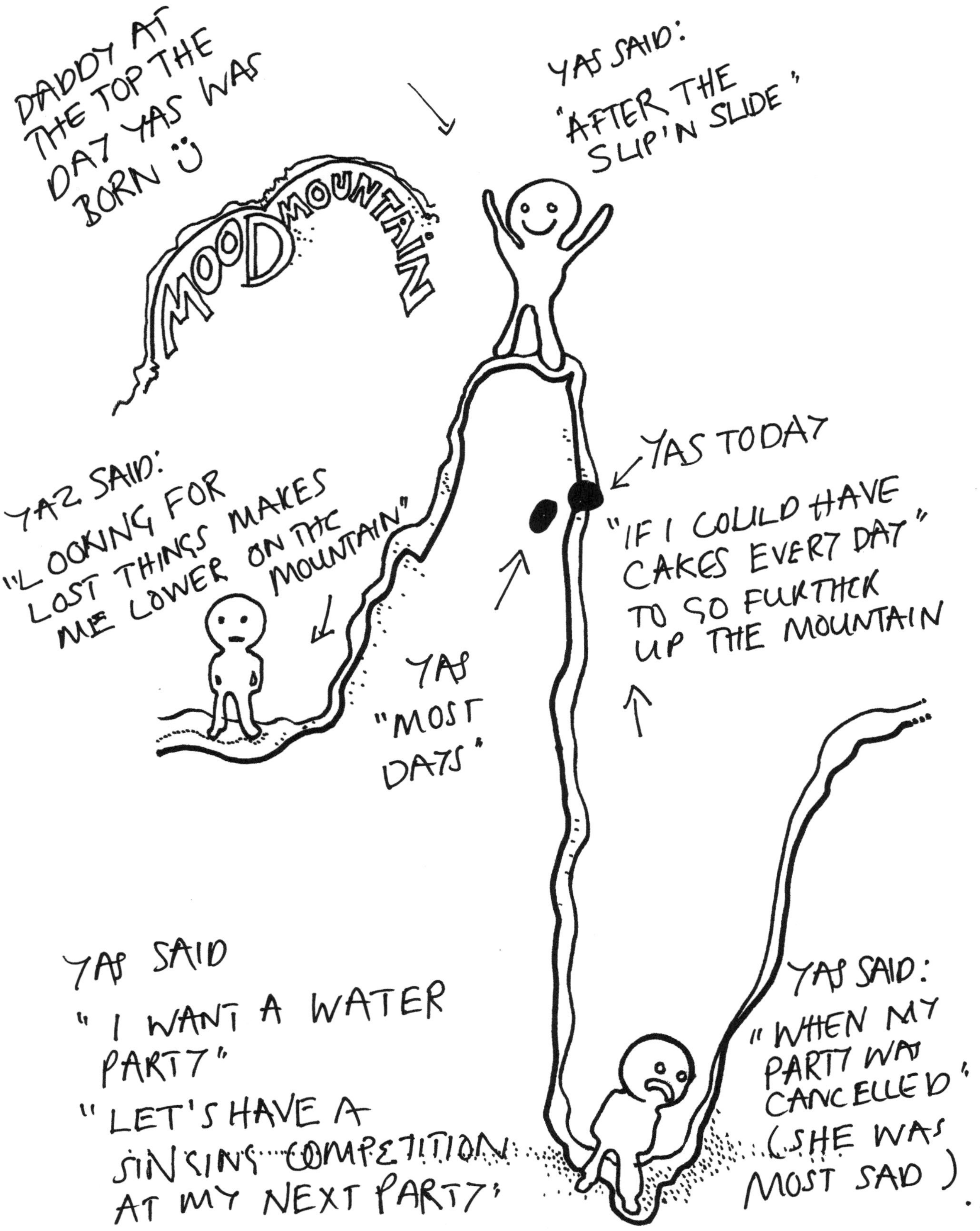
DADDY AT THE TOP THE DAY YAS WAS BORN :)
MOOD MOUNTAIN
YAS SAID:
"AFTER THE SLIP'N SLIDE"
YAZ SAID:
"LOOKING FOR LOST THINGS MAKES ME LOWER ON THE MOUNTAIN"
YAS TODAY
"IF I COULD HAVE CAKES EVERY DAY"
TO GO FURTHER UP THE MOUNTAIN
YAS
"MOST DAYS"
YAS SAID
"I WANT A WATER PARTY"
"LET'S HAVE A SINGING COMPETITION AT MY NEXT PARTY"
YAS SAID:
"WHEN MY PARTY WAS CANCELLED" (SHE WAS MOST SAD).

MAY 2021.

How are you? Mood Mountain

Sometimes it's hard to describe how you feel. This is an easy way to describe where you are at today, without saying a word.
Margo, Ian and Virginia – Mood Mountain

Margo the Magnificent is full of life and brims with creativity. She might well be the president of the world one day; such is her vision. As the youngest of all these Incredible kids, her capacity to grasp the idea of Mood Mountain was admirable. At first Margo was worried about what sort of mark she should make. Her dad, Ian, with reassuring calm, let her choose whatever mark she wanted and then she felt confident enough to have a go. Both Virginia (her mum) and Ian joined in this conversation, which is likely to make the event really special for her (see 'It's a Work in Progress: Primary/elementary school-age children are primed to learn from you, to be around you').

Margo's high point was playing with the pirate ships at school and the last time she felt like she was in the pit was 'when (a classmate) did a mean face' to her. Ian commented that sounded difficult and asked more about it. Taking time to stop to hear the hard things that happen in your child's life is a great bonding opportunity (see 'Top Tips: Tough times? Climb into the pit with your child'). Virginia began to share her best and worst times which Margo found really engaging. One of her mum's comments reminded her of a good time they had had together, and Margo chimed in 'Oh yes, me too!' We suggest inviting your child to host a conversation or two so that there is a chance for parents to share and model communication skills (see 'Pick 'n' Mix') but here intuitively Margo picked up the ideas and began to ask more about her mum's experiences and they discussed together how tough it had been missing extended family during lockdown. Margo said she 'felt happy' doing Mood Mountain. With that conversation done, she asked 'What's next?' She is *on it*.

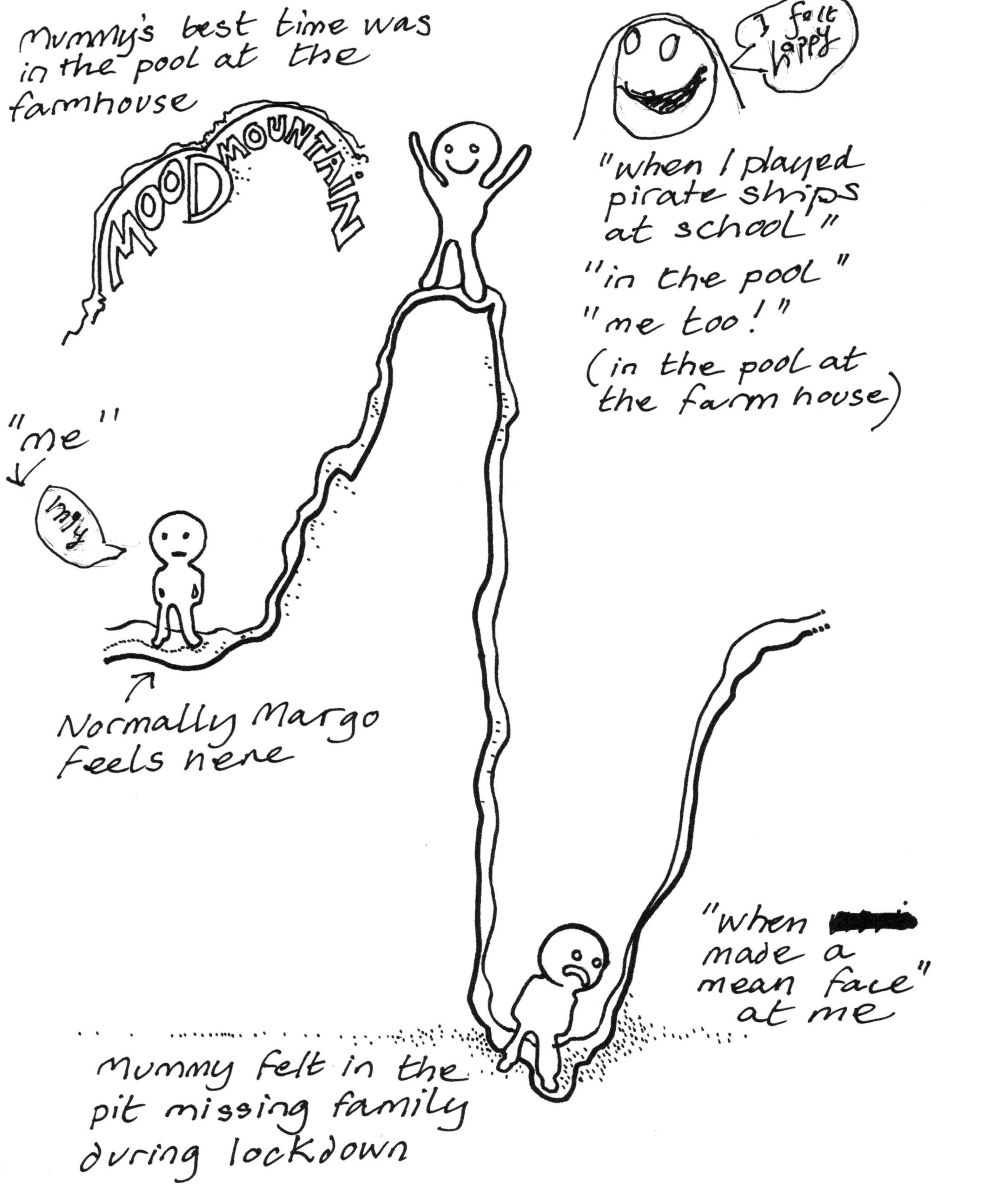

How are you? Heads and Hearts – Step 1

This is all about figuring out the difference between thoughts and feelings. It is great practice for worriers.

Nadia and Hanna – Heads and Hearts

Nadia is 12 years old. She loves dance and animals. If it's got fur and big ears, she's a fan. She is known for her kindness to other people as well as her furry friends. She has a tendency to worry and recently has been worrying so much about her ballet exam that she hasn't been sleeping well, so she and her mum, Hanna, tried out the Heads and Hearts conversations.

Hanna was really keen to give the conversations a go, much keener than Nadia at first. She said she had to sit on her urge to try a conversation and wait until it felt okay for Nadia or else she might feel overwhelmed. Hanna said wryly 'I worry about how much Nadia worries' (see 'Top Tips: Calm brains communicate best'). It was difficult to figure out the difference between thoughts and feelings. Nadia said, 'At first I put "I am going to fail my ballet exam" in the heart but then we figured out it's actually a thought.' This is a really common experience and this conversation idea does take a lot of practice (see Chapter 2, 'It's A Work in Progress: Conversation and relationship building takes time to learn, just like any skill').

HEADS AND HEARTS

How are you? Heads and Hearts – Step 2

This conversation introduces the idea that we can decide how we feel, because we can change what we think.
Nadia and Hanna – Heads and Hearts

Nadia and Hanna took Nadia's thought 'I'm going to fail my ballet exam' and tried it out in Step 2. This is advanced stuff (and remember Nadia is the oldest in the Incredible group). You can see how well Nadia and Hanna did, but it took a lot of discussion together. You may well find that this particular technique is not for you or your child may be too young, so if Step 1 is a struggle, leave it for a bit and come back to it in a few months.

Hanna said it took some time to figure out a different thought about the ballet exam. At first Nadia kept saying 'But what if I fail?' which they both realized was a similar thought to 'I'm going to fail my ballet exam' but dressed up in a slightly different way. Hanna commented, 'As we were talking, I asked what would happen if she *did* fail and then she hit on the re-sit idea.' This is an example of first-rate conversation skills. Hanna waited and gave Nadia space to think it through herself and asked some questions which helped her get unstuck, rather than diving in and offering an answer. Notice that this conversation might not actually change feelings in the moment, it just introduces *the idea* that you can change a feeling if you can just change the thought.

They have been trying to do the thought-changing conversations in Heads and Hearts – Step 2 on the way to school because that's when Nadia's worries tend to appear (see 'Top Tips: Look after spontaneous communications – they are valuable'). Nadia said, 'I didn't really think it would make much difference, but once Mum and I began to talk and use the thought-changing bubbles, I really got it...I passed my ballet exam, by the way!'

HEADS AND HEARTS

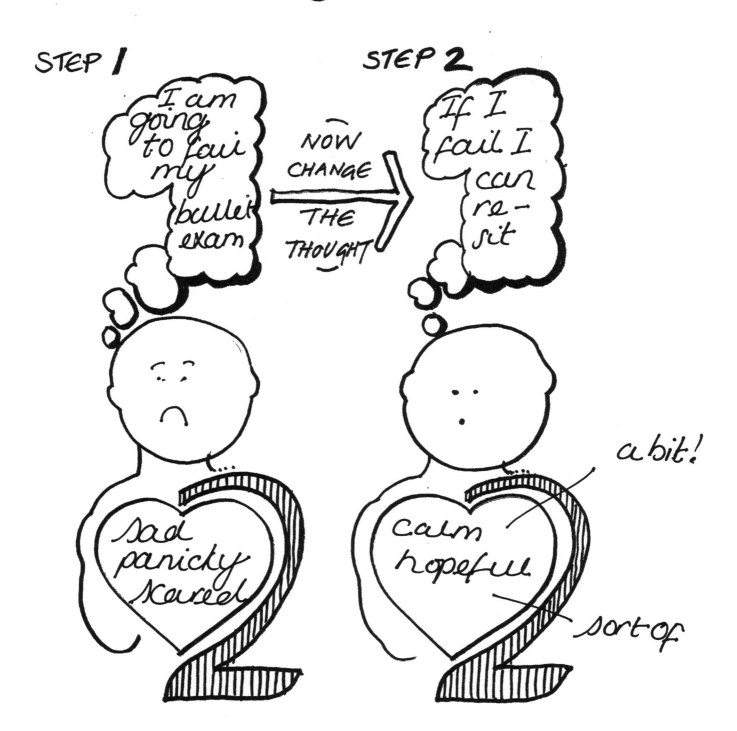

What helps? Support Squad

This conversation is about figuring out the VIPs in a child's life – particularly trusted adults and friends. It highlights social support, safety nets and friendships.

Imogen and Laura – Support Squad

Imogen is 5 years old, so one of the youngest in our Incredible group. She scooters like a pro and draws beautifully, as you can see from her picture. (She chose the most vibrant colours for her drawing, which we can't reproduce here.) This is an extraordinarily careful drawing for someone so young. In this case, Imogen enjoyed doing the little details of each person she named in her squad so the drawing became part of the conversation, but your situation might be different. Some kids might draw an initial or ask you to write the names of the squad, it's all valuable (see 'It's a Work in Progress: Using visual material...'). Imogen's support squad included a much-loved toy and a wide range of friends and relatives. She said that she could have added many more to her squad if she had had more room. You can always add an extension page if your child feels that important people have been missed.

Imogen's mum, Laura, describes home-schooling during lockdown as a really useful experience because she learnt that going at Imogen's pace and picking up the signs when she had had enough (even if the job wasn't quite finished) really helped them go forward. These 'sensitivity' skills are the bedrock of great parenting (see 'Top Tips: Read the room') and it shows in the way her mum described their Incredible Conversation experience: 'It was relaxed, and we chatted (as she drew).' Laura commented that she enjoyed taking the time out together to think together. And Imogen's verdict? 'When can we do it again?'

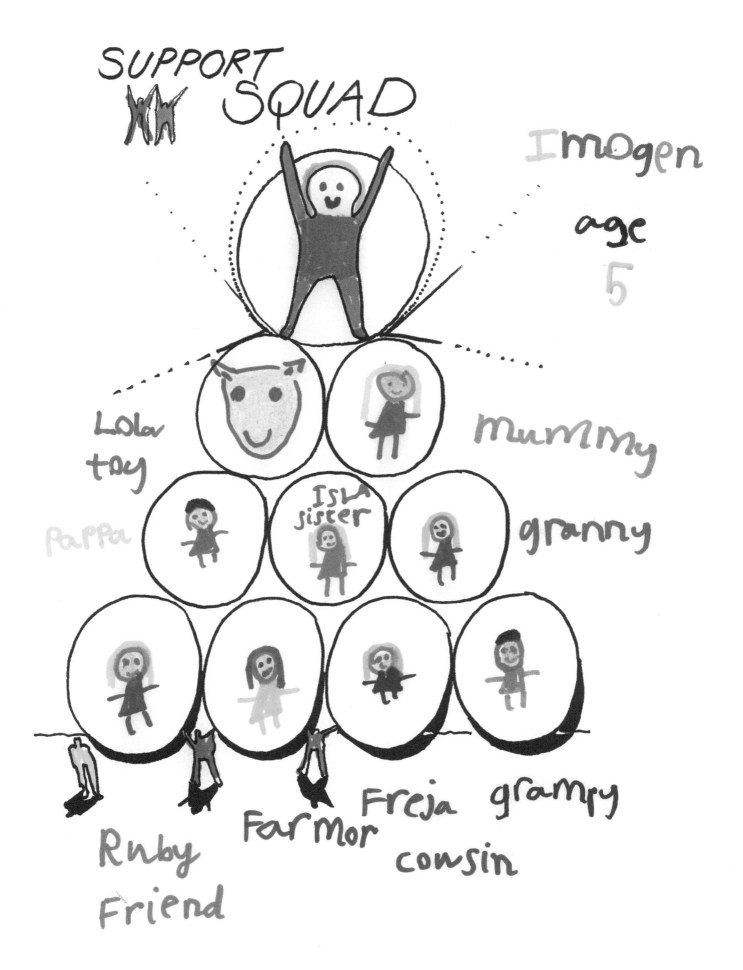

What gets in the way? Muddle and Make Up

Discussing a time when family life got in a muddle (like a row) and figuring out – after the storm has passed – how it got sorted, is healing. If your family find arguments get in the way a lot, this one is for you.

Jaden and Grace – Muddle and Make Up

Jaden is 9. He loves drawing but doesn't love homework much at all. Jaden's mum, Grace, is a generous character, always open to new ideas and worries that she and Jaden don't connect because he is 'always on the go'. They both agree that there are a lot of raised voices in their family, but there is also a lot of love. Grace said she could feel him back out of the room when she showed him the book, so she told him it was 'about drawing' which was a brilliant idea because drawing has great associations for him but written work is often linked to rows in the family (see 'Top Tips: A reluctant participant? Any bad associations with a paper and pen?'). 'Ask me to draw and I'm happy,' said Jaden. This is a good example of using the conversation pages in any way that works for your family. Grace did the writing and Jaden did the drawing on Muddle and Make Up.

They chose to talk about getting in a muddle over stopping screens to do homework. Rather cleverly, Jaden's mum had this conversation during the school holidays when homework rows were not an issue. Talking about a row is a good idea but it's important to wait until everyone involved has calmed down (see 'Top Tips: Calm brains communicate best'). Jaden commented, 'I thought it was cool to draw an argument. I've never done that before.' They both said the best bit of the conversation was giving each other tips. Jaden said he needed some warning before stopping his gaming so he could bank his wins and Grace's tip was that they would start homework at the same time each day. These tips are brilliant stuff, because with an agreed start time, Jaden can plan his gaming better, there is no room for debate and so less chance of emotions running high.

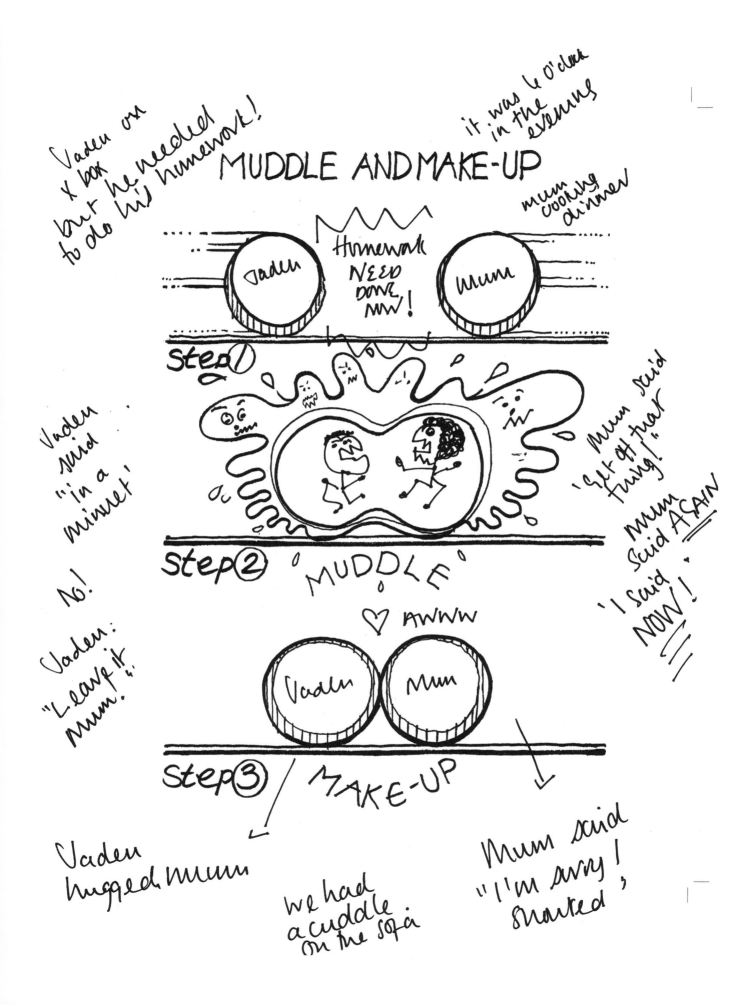

Appendix 2

Conversation Pathways

WHO ARE YOU?

BLOWING BUBBLES

PIECE OF CAKE

HOW ARE YOU?

HEADS & HEARTS 1

HEADS & HEARTS 2

WHAT HELPS YOU?

HELPING HANDS

STEPPING STONES

POWER UP

WHAT GETS IN THE WAY

UH-OH SPOILER ALERT

ROAD BLOCKS

IF YOUR KIDS TEND TO WORRY, TRY THESE INCREDIBLE CONVERSATIONS

WHO ARE YOU?

MEMORY FRAME GAME

HOW ARE YOU?

WORRY POTS

WHAT HELPS YOU?

POWER UP

WHAT GETS IN THE WAY?

WHAT IF-FING

WHO ARE YOU?

PIECE OF CAKE

HOW ARE YOU?

HEADS & HEARTS

WHAT HELPS YOU?

HELPING HANDS

STEPPING STONES

WHAT GETS IN THE WAY?

OOPS LOOPS

MUDDLE & MAKE·UP

UH-OH... SPOILER ALERT

Further Reading

Brown, B. (2013) *The Gifts of Imperfect Parenting: Raising Children with Courage, Compassion and Connection*. Audiobook. Louisville, CO: Sounds True, Inc.

Davidson, R. (2019) on compassion. Listen to him talking on the podcast *On Being* with Krista Tippett: https://onbeing.org/programs/richard-davidson-a-neuroscientist-on-love-and-learning-feb2019.

Feldman Barrett, L. (2018) *How Emotions Are Made: The Secret Life of the Brain*. London: Pan MacMillan.

Fonagy, P. (2018) *Attachment Theory and Psychoanalysis*. Abingdon: Routledge.

Gopnik, A. (2017) *The Gardener and the Carpenter: What the New Science of Child Development Tells Us About the Relationship between Parents and Children*. Vintage Digital.

Harter, S. (1999) *The Construction of the Self: A Developmental Perspective*. New York, NY: Guilford Press.

Hohnen, B., Gilmour, J. and Murphy, T. (2019) *The Incredible Teenage Brain: Everything You Need to Know To Unlock Your Teen's Potential*. London: Jessica Kingsley Publishers.

Perry, P. (2020) *The Book You Wish Your Parents Had Read (and Your Children Will Be Glad That You Did)*. London: Penguin Life.

Rogers, C. (1951) *Client-Centered Therapy: Its Current Practice, Implications and Theory*. London: Constable.

Selye, H. (1956) *The Stress of Life*. New York, NY: McGraw-Hill Book Company.

Siegel, D. (2013) *Parenting from the Inside Out: How a Deeper Self-Understanding Can Help You Raise Children Who Thrive*. New York, NY: Tarcher Perigee.

Skinner, E.A. and Zimmer-Gembeck, J. (2016) *The Development of Coping: Stress, Neurophysiology, Social Relationships, and Resilience During Childhood and Adolescence*. New York, NY: Springer.

White, M. (2007) *Maps of Narrative Practice*. New York, NY: W.W. Norton & Co.

Index

Other JKP books

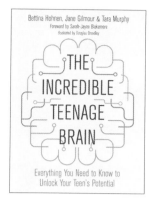

The Incredible Teenage Brain
Everything You Need to Know to Unlock Your Teen's Potential
Bettina Hohnen, Jane Gilmour and Tara Murphy

£15.99 | $21.95 | PB | 360PP | ISBN 978 1 78592 557 3 |
eISBN 978 1 78450 952 1

This book is a must-read for anyone parenting, teaching or supporting teens who wants to empower them to reach their potential. Written by a team of clinical psychologists, it leads you through tried-and-tested strategies to build strong relationships and improve communication with young people as they develop, learn and grow.

In the book we learn that the 'teenage brain' is unique, which gives us an incredible opportunity for change and development, but it is also a time when young people are particularly sensitive and potentially vulnerable. It guides you through ways to communicate effectively with teens without negatively affecting their self-esteem. There are plenty of tips about what to say, what not say and the best mindset to use with teens, day to day.

The authors draw from the latest research in neuroscience and psychology, years of clinical expertise and first-hand parenting experience. It's relatable like your best friend's advice, and informed by scientific evidence – easy to read, hard to put down.

Bettina, Jane and Tara are clinical psychologists who have a specialist interest in neuropsychology and are all based at or have worked at Great Ormond Street Hospital and University College London. All have academic backgrounds and over 20 years' experience working with children, young people and families, and delivering training to parents and professionals.

Creative Ways to Help Children Manage BIG Feelings
A Therapist's Guide to Working with Preschool and Primary Children
Dr Fiona Zandt and Dr Suzanne Barrett
Foreword by Associate Professor Lesley Bretherton

£19.99 | $29.95 | PB | 200PP | ISBN 978 1 78592 074 5 |
eISBN 978 1 78450 487 8

Help children to stay on top of 'big' feelings like anger, sadness and anxiety with this ingeniously easy-to-use therapy toolkit. Focusing on making therapy for children both purposeful and playful, the book provides 47 activities to transform your sessions using everyday materials and a variety of tried-and-tested therapy models.

The authors deliver sage advice on how to work with children, adapting your approach for different age groups and judging how and when to involve parents and teachers. The handy reference table allows you to quickly fish out the perfect activity for the moment, according to the emotion the child is experiencing, or the therapeutic method needed. With its winning mix of creative resources and clinical expertise, all wrapped up in a simple and practical format, this is the ideal companion for both new and experienced therapists working with children aged 4–12.

Dr Fiona Zandt is a clinical psychologist who currently works at the Royal Children's Hospital and has a successful private practice in Melbourne. She has over 15 years' experience working with children and families with a broad range of psychological difficulties.

Dr Suzanne Barrett is a clinical psychologist who has over 17 years' experience working therapeutically with children and families as well as significant experience in training and supervising psychologists working with children. She previously worked for the Royal Children's Hospital Mental Health Service, and now has a successful private practice in Melbourne.

Creative Ways to Help Children Manage Anxiety
Ideas and Activities for Working Therapeutically with Worried
Children and Their Families
Dr Fiona Zandt and Dr Suzanne Barrett
Foreword by Dr Karen Cassiday

£19.99 | $27.95 | PB | 208PP | ISBN 978 1 78775 094 4 |
eISBN 978 1 78775 095 1

This book sets out therapeutic activities to help children aged 4–12 years and their families to better understand and manage anxiety. It explains how to work with anxious children, providing a framework for assessment and therapy that draws on CBT, ACT and narrative therapy approaches. Lots of practical tips for therapists are included and important developmental considerations are discussed, including adapting therapy for children with developmental difficulties, and working with families and schools.

Over 50 playful therapeutic activities are included, which have been developed through the authors' extensive work with children, giving children an arsenal of coping strategies. They focus on key areas such as understanding anxiety, managing anxious thoughts, and building resilience and use readily available, inexpensive materials and downloadable templates which are provided in the book. This is the perfect tool for therapists looking for playful and purposeful ways to work with children with anxiety.

Dr Fiona Zandt is a clinical psychologist who currently works at the Royal Children's Hospital and has a successful private practice in Melbourne. She has over 15 years' experience working with children and families with a broad range of psychological difficulties.

Dr Suzanne Barrett is a clinical psychologist who has over 17 years' experience working therapeutically with children and families as well as significant experience in training and supervising psychologists working with children. She previously worked for the Royal Children's Hospital Mental Health Service, and now has a successful private practice in Melbourne.

CBT Doodling for Kids

50 Illustrated Handouts to Help Build Confidence and Emotional
Resilience in Children Aged 6–11
Tanja Sharpe

£17.99 | $24.95 | PB | 112PP | ISBN 978 1 78592 537 5 | eISBN 978 1 78775 017 3

Using creative therapy techniques developed through years of working with young children, this activity book will be an invaluable resource for professionals working with children aged 6–11. Unique drawing exercises develop confidence, encourage self-awareness and help open up conversations where children are struggling to verbalize their thoughts or emotions.

In this interactive book, 50 illustrated, entertaining characters help children explore and process their emotions – such as Stomper who loves to dance, or the Balloon Brothers who lift away sad feelings. These tried-and-tested communication tools are particularly helpful for children with autism or additional needs, or children suffering from anxiety or bullying.

Each illustrated character is accompanied by a fully photocopiable story page to guide discussions. With additional information for counsellors, this book will be an invaluable tool for therapists, social workers, SENCOs and educational professionals.

Tanja Sharpe is a qualified creative therapist. She specialises in CBT and mindfulness therapy for children with autism or special needs. Tanja runs creative therapy training courses and founded the Creative Counsellors Club.